The Greatest French Food Book in the World

✦

Jerome Lord

Published by Humble Pie Publishing,
Palm Beach, FL, 33480

ISBN: 061551300X
ISBN 13: 9780615513003

Library of Congress Control Number: 2011934337
CreateSpace, North Charleston, SC

Dedication

I want to dedicate this book with affection, respect and
thanksgiving to my family and friends who contributed
in many different ways to this book:

Eleanor Louise de Peverel duBarry FitzWarin Collins Lord

✦

Hayes Alexander FitzWarin Lord
Maria Yip Lord
Stavely Hampston deHodnet Lord
Savile Collins de Montenay Lord
Dorian Warfield d'Amours Lord
Wallis Jennings de Pantulf Lord-Hart
Andrew Richard Hart
Hayes Li Collins Lord

✦

William Thomas Keavy, R.I.P.
David George Scannell
Francois Minot

Acknowledgments

I want to thank Dennis Reed, who added so greatly to my sanity as this book was being prepared for publishing. He had already fixed my computer completely in one day after the Geek Squad had consistently failed do so over a period of three months, thus enabling me to restart my work. He was also the principal technical architect and sometime editor of the final document going to the publishers. Just prior to this adventure, John Bartoldus had not only enlarged my electronic capability over a period of previous months, but had also painstakingly walked me through a number of important repairs and improvements. He proved to be a patient and awe-inspiring teacher and enabler. I owe both of these gifted men a permanent place in the Lord Hall of Fame.

I also want to recognize the very talented François Minot, late of the Lion d'Or in Saulieu, France. His gift for creating French food was my greatest prompt to write this affectionate book. Wherever you are, Francois, I am still grateful to you for the very best luncheon I have ever had in all of France.

Over the years I have held wonderfully formative conversations with Escoffier, Carême, Le Nôtre, and Bocuse as I stopped by to critique their superb food. These conversations were inspiring, and helped me to understand even better than I did the enormous value of the criticisms and the praise that I brought to their work. For example, Le Notre gave me as a gift of gratitude the flour that was left over when he was baking a Gateau Mouche.

And my great thanks to the following citizens of France who have inspired me at various stages of my life to "think France": Alyette Onnis, Comtesse de Montenay and Dr. Daniele Onnis ; Albane and Cyrille, Vicomte and Vicomtesse de Beaurepaire; Xavier Boivin-Champeau; Guarin de Metz; Brigitte Bardot; Georges Bizet; Patachou; Yves Neveux; Alexandre Dumas; Alain Delon; Simone Signoret; Geoffroy de Pinoncely; Francois Truffaut; Henri-Cécile, Duc du Dubonnet; Jean-Pierre Léaud; Loulou de la Falaise; François Mitterand; Anna Pacquin; Georges Sand; Pistache de Bruit; and Alumette de Vavasour.

I am also grateful to the French Minister for Cultural Affairs, Andre Gide, and to the French Government for their very kind offer to publish this book in Latin – an offer that I have mostly declined.

JEL

About the Author

We asked Jerome Lord to tell us something about himself. Although we are sure he knows English, he responded in Tagalog. Something about "patterned baldness." Since none of us really has a command of Tagalog, at least not in the original, we asked elsewhere about him. Understandably, some of the replies are unprintable. A few weren't :

Jamie Crassman, a professional newcomer: "I think he is a man who has suffered the sticks and stones of outrageous bones, but I'm not 100% sure, as I have never met him."

Larry King, professional larynx: "I think he was on my Sunday morning Sunrise Service Program in Phoenix, ...yeah, that's right. ...we thought it was strange, because he's partly an atheist."

Whoopee Porcelain: "Wasn't he the guy who kept coming back to the Almost Cleaners on Grove Street, trying to get the owner to put the spots back on his suit because he thought they gave it more character?"

Melanania Melanov, the author's psychotherapist : "I only know a few facts about him, like he is in Who's Who in the World and things like that. But I know a great deal about his dreams and his neuroses. Just ask me. But it'll cost you."

Jerome Lord: "Nobody can do me the way I can do me. But my social circles and acquaintances are few, so there is always the possibility that someone else can do me better than I can."

Igor Stravinsky, lumberjack and composer: "Believe me, knowing him is like knowing too much about something."

Trelawnie Zither, retired mortician: "His being alive is a dishonor to his memory."

Chlorina Lox Hither, hair-lengthening expert: "I know at Georgetown he headed up a secret radical group called The Chimes. Still, he's the only Jerome I know whose name is pronounced Jair-um and not Je-Rome. I don't know why, but if you find out, keep it to yourself."

Stephen King: "This book is sheer genius. Its author is a genius, and we should welcome his forthcoming institutionalization so that we can preserve his genius intact. The only flaws I could find were in the language and the ideas."

Preface

No one will ever fully understand the pain of creating something immortal out of whole cloth, like this priceless book. I know I certainly won't, because I never had a single pain while creating it. Perhaps this can be explained by a simple fact of my life: I suffer from such an incredible sense of boredom that my mind usually fills the vacuum with a marmalade made from gooseberries. Anyone who is familiar with the rhapsodies of gooseberry marmalade already knows that it confers upon the bored brain a listlessness akin to The Sleep That Outsleeps Rip van Winkle.

I discovered at age seven that the antidote for this listlessness is French Food. Writing about French Food induces a wakefulness that transcends the cheeks and opens the eyebrows. Having twice read before the age of eight all 3247 pages of the Larousse Gastronomique, I began to write about French food immediately thereafter. This may account for the amputational misery of my handwriting. (It should be noted that I write before I eat, and in that order.)

Larousse himself learned of my ambitious undertaking, and sent his dear wife Theophila to the United States to investigate. After reading a few instructive chapters of mine, Theo telegrammed him, and he flew over. (Yes, it was during this trip that Larousse became addicted to hotdogs *and* hamburgers, and on their buns. It took all the pressure the Académie Française Culinaire could bring to bear to convince him not to include these American delicacies in the newest edition of his tome).

When he saw the progress I was making, Larousse begged me; if I was going to write a book about French food in English, would I at least write it with a French accent. Not knowing exactly what he meant, I instantly wanted to agree.

But I demurred, as only an eight-year-old can demur, though it is in fact harder to demur in French, and it took me three tries before I got it wrong. But write I did, and even the insanely jealous citizens of France could not deny me the honor to which I was entitled by sheer force of talent. Thus I am the only American to have been honored with the food equivalent of the Croix de Guerre, namely, the Langue Rouge de la Faison (The Pheasant's Red Tongue), which is France's highest honor in the realm of 8-year-olds.

Inevitably, the très petits bourgeois of France, commanded by the Nationalist Party, although unable to deny me my honors, raised unholy havoc at this intrusion of an *American* child into the ranks of France's most cherished royalty. So I flew to France and took the three-week taste test at the Académie Académique et Scolaire de la Haute Cuisine Française and I was honored, though not surprised, to receive 10.94 of a possible 10, thereby scoring higher than had any other French food writer/critic in the past 212 years, or maybe even 213. After that, the très petits bourgeois pointed me out to their children in the streets of Paris and Lyon as a role-model, an icon of taste and accomplishment.

Now you'll see why.

Jerome Lord

Introduction

It's remarkable how the lessons of history teach us so many lessons of history. If it were not for the sacrosanct nature of history, one might be induced to forget that our history is the one thing we get to outlive. For American readers, of course, who have about as much trouble reading English as anyone else, the history of French food might seem too European, except when it's written in English.

In that case, the history of French food might be considered inedible, except for the fact that we Americans have a special ability to ignore all of history while eating every kind of food. We did it when we ate dinner with the Indians at the first Thanksgiving; and we have been ignoring history ever since, while stuffing ourselves into eternity. It's definitely the American way. We are the fat people of the Universe.

This then will be a book you will want to put down even before you pick it up. It is far too amusing and provocative for a person like you, who wants to put down books before picking them up, and it is far too rewarding with the kind of misinformation that has evaded you since birth.

On second thought, I think it would do you good to pick up this book. Then at least you will remember the title when every cocktail party, dinner party, and congregation of cognoscenti will echo with conversation about the book you were just about to put down before you picked it up. You certainly don't want the cognoscenti to think you're a boor before you even open your mouth, at which point they will see that their suspicions are up for grabs.

So listen to all those cocktail party conversations about The Greatest French Food Book in the World. You'll be glad you did or you didn't.

Jerome Lord

Table of Contents

I

An Early Afterthought

As soon as you saw the title of this book, a shiver of excitement probably shot up your leg, across your abdomen, through your digestive juices and straight into the pituitary gland, which, as medical and culinary science now affirm, is the French food center of the nervous system. This particular shiver is a normal response, and, you should welcome it. It is not, as some might think, a reminiscence of sciatica, or even an apprehension of varicose veins. It is the spontaneous hunger pain that traditionally accompanies the subject of French food, and is the first and very best sign that you are really ready for this book.

Of course, to be perfectly fair about it, no one is ever quite as ready for this book as a hunger pain would suggest, not even the author. For when it comes to French food, the one thing we all have in common is that we are all French food novices, even the French. Nor could it be otherwise. French Food is not only an ancient and honorable subject, but we now know that it was around for many centuries before anyone thought of cooking it.

So clearly we are at a great historical disadvantage, and we had better realize that fact right off. In other words, the worst mistake this book could make would be to ignore your amateur status and dump you right into the middle of French food, where you would have to sink or swim for yourself. No, I repeat: we are novices all, and should you put down this book right now, never to take it up again, you will at least have had the satisfaction of knowing that, whoever you are and wherever you live, you will be among equally ignorant friends for the rest of your life.

Should you, on the other hand, decide to cast all caution to the wind and keep on reading, then let it be said for your enjoyment and self-esteem that there are a lot of food historians at work nowadays, and any of them will tell you that French food novices are as old as French food itself. Even more happily, recent research has shown that one out of every two French food novices is an American. This means that the average American French food novice, traditionally younger than his French counterpart, has a much shorter walk to the nearest novice than does the average novice in places like Nepal and Kazakhstan.

While this will be bad news for American podiatrists, the rest of you can relax a little, knowing that here in the United States you are virtually surrounded by French food novices. You might also feel better if you asked yourself whether you would feel comfortable being a novice who already has a lot of experience. If so, you would then have to ask yourself whether you felt there was anything very attractive about people we might call seasoned novices.

Trusting that the answer would be a firm "No!" we can now proceed to show throughout the remainder of this book that the admission of almost total ignorance is the key to French food. It is always possible, however, that you do not know exactly how ignorant you really are. If there is no one in your immediate circle of relatives and friends willing to tell you, you might be tempted to say something skittish; you might, for example, relate any ignorance on your part to the lifelong immaturity of your eating habits, or to your father's conviction that everything the French eat comes out of an aquarium. Or you might say that you have been overwhelmed by Hector Peridot's famous dictum, "Once a French citizen has eaten with authority for two or three years, always a citizen." and are no longer able to deal with the dimensions of your own ignorance.

To these and other variations of the skittish, we now offer the perfect solution. If you think you are a French food novice, but you entertain a reasonable doubt, (even if that doubt gives you some pleasure) then all you have to do is take another look at the price of this book. It should persuade you that you are very much a novice, and could hardly afford to be otherwise.

Now that the pressure to be knowledgeable is off, you can confidently march up to the cashier, pay the asking price, and walk out of the store with this book, proudly unwrapped, tucked under your chin for all to see. If by chance you have already bought it, you can now take it out of its plain brown wrapper and leave the bathroom. In short, you need no longer apologize. You have finally got it: The Greatest French Food Book in the World, here at last to take French food out of the fat and into the fire.

Whatever else it ends up doing, (and at this point your guess is as good as mine) this book will take the wraps off French food. It will unravel all the yarns. It will plumb the unfathomables. It will reveal all the exotics, disassemble the manageables, and ignite the recipes. Eventually, it may even sweep French food right off its feet and into your lap. In any case, of this you can be sure: by the time you are finished with this book, you will have come to the end of French food.

II

Some More Early Afterthoughts

By this time, reviewers will be pulling their pens out and racking their brains for a few descriptives. Conscious of their needs, and anxious to abet them, we want to offer a few comments on the nature of this book so that those who need to can stop here.

The Greatest French Food Book in the World (GFFBITW) is both a catechism and an encyclopedia. To some, it will seem a new beginning, while to others it will seem the complete end. But no matter at which point along the French food spectrum you eat, this book is bound to take your breath away, for it has the dramatic scope of the Bible, the sweet winsome of Winnie-the-Pooh, and the kind of majestic authority one would expect to find in an autobiography of God the Father.[1] Nor could it be anything less, for you to have a right to expect both greatness and humility from a book that dares to tell the French food story.

Many people, and particularly the initiated, will be surprised by the thinness of this book. "It can't be much of a story," they will say. Their expectation that a French food book must be grossly overweight is a bias centering around the popular misconception that quantity is equal to the sum of its parts. The author and the publishers feel quite differently about it. We feel a thin French food book has many advantages.

It will help explode the myth that fat people read too much, or that food people only read dictionaries, or that their readers are all French. It will prove to the Italians once and for all that they can take pasta out of their breakfasts and still have a morning newspaper. It will show Ernest Hemingway fans that a small book can be nourishing without being out of print. Above all, it will decisively prove that the most sophisticated cuisine in Europe can be held in two hands.

The GFFB in the W is a food book, not a cookbook. A food book is different from a cookbook in the following ways: (1) it is characterized by the absence of work. (2) It contains no recipes whatsoever. (3) The food stains on the inside pages are bogus. (4) It contains the fewest possible instructions on doing anything whatsoever with food —(even preparing, assembling, battling and defrosting)— and what few instructions there are have been included solely to keep busy hands so light they would make idle work. (5) It contains none of those food photographs designed to show you how something could have looked if you had only done it right.

---

1 This is not to be confused with God the Son or God the Holy Spirit, who will be the separate subjects of the second and third volumes in the anthology about to be published in an Authoritative Series by the Episcopalians.

We realize we are running a risk by keeping this book thin. Somewhere there is a wit who will claim that here at last is the Flyweight of French food books. But as you read on, after the first few rounds you will find it is at least a Bantamweight, and by the time you have gone the whole round, the book will probably qualify as a heavyweight.

Thin or fat, young or old, — does it really matter? As the French always remind us, true beauty is in the eyes of the face, and the really beautiful thing about this book is its determination to tell the whole truth about French food, and nothing but the whole. In its desperation, French food cries out for a voice in the wilderness, and the author is pleased to believe you will hear it right here.

Cookbooks, on the other hand, are the handmaiden of French food novices. The most famous is the corpulent Larousse Gastronomique, the best-selling volume by Auguste Gastronomique, brother of the veterate traveler and himself a dauntless, who came to the United States in 1813 and spent four years transcribing the original Fanny Farmer Cook Book into the metric system before secretly carrying the whole manuscript out of the country.

The Larousse has many peculiarities that may, or may not, advertise it to readers who already find themselves leaning toward food books. For example, it has within its pages the world's largest and tastiest collection of dead binding bugs. And it refuses to be literal about cooking. Instead of showing a fully prepared lobster in Aspic with trout fins, it will only prescribe the shade of red to which the lobster's feelers should be poached. In short, the Larousse (which in French means 'Larousse') grinds out a lot of cooking problems.

But to really understand why a cookbook presents all French food novices with almost uncookable problems, you first have to know something about French fun. It is true that the French deserve most of the credit for putting the fun back into food. This was no accident. (The French do not have accidents because it is far too small a country.) In French food, the fun is almost all on purpose.

Of course, like civilized people everywhere, the French do not have their fun all at once, in a purge. Nor do they put all their fun into very select foods that might inspire the remark: "Oh God, but I really do think a meadowlark is a fun food." No, the French secret is that they steep themselves slowly in fun, starting with an askance, and then a double-take, and then a lip-curl, and then an eyebrow arch, and then a pair of flared nostrils, and then a heh, and another heh, and then the ha, and the ha, ha, and the triple ha, with a ho, or a double ho, or a hee, or a hee hee, or a hee 4, and on, and on, down the pancreas and into the epidemic, shaking the whole works. If you have to wait an excruciatingly long time for the French to have all their fun, it is certainly worth their wait.

The basic laugh in French food is that classic French recipes have no ending. Some of these recipes carry you right to the door of the oven and then leave you there to test your mettle for yourself. Others either get you half-way through the beating or a third of the way through a beautiful basting, and then, when you turn the page, you find you are left to beat and baste for yourself. The recipes of the classic French cookbook, therefore, represent a style of cooking as ingenious as it is disarming, with all the charm of an author who refuses to give you the final chapter of a murder-mystery.

This fun, or "unfinished," approach to the preparation of food has its margin of error. Even a minor misstep, or an almost perfect guess, can lead to tragic endings, as when a turkey Florentine suddenly dismembers into an omelette of cranberries, or when a *gâteau de noix,* (the nut cake that traditionally is offered in celebration of the architecture of France's deadly Maginot Line) rises well past its bedtime into a soufflé.

Nevertheless, the challenge of finishing on your own terms what has begun on someone else's terms, which is very French, is an energetic, for it lets a cook test himself under fire to see how good are his analytical glands, his powers of elevation, his innards, and his outbasket. In short, this is the "Have You Tasted My Finale?" School of food creation, with so many rules and so much artistry that French cooking has become a sort of lycée-at-home, in which every kitchen is a schoolhouse and every student gets to eat the daily quiz. Some would call the unfinished recipe France's most enviable response to the possibilities of extension education.

III

The Birth of the GFFBIW

If you are like all of the other readers who have gotten this far, you will have come to the point where you want to know something about the creation of this book. The story is an inspiring one, destined forever to be repeated in the re-telling. It happened that, prior to the time he became publisher of this book, the publisher of this book was on one of these long, peaceful visits to France that tend so successfully to distill the piss out of the vinegar in your bile duct while emptying your liver of all excess Vitamin B12.

As he wandered about the French countryside, he noticed a consistent characteristic of French domiciles, whether house or hotel: each had several shelves of books on the art of French cooking. He also noticed that many of the books were one hundred or more years old, and this surprised him, for he realized how very recently French food had become popular in France. He meditated upon this apparent contradiction and finally supined that other countries, where French cuisine had long been popular without benefit of support from the printed word, ought to be rewarded with a French food book.

The idea began to excite him, for he is the sort of man who carries on his business with what admirers are wont to call a Ringling Brothers syndrome; that is, he tends to like books that are just one surprise after another, full of hairy things that bounce, with pastries covering the footnotes, sequins on the sleeve, and a unique combination of aromas that lingers in the nose for the rest of your life. He has always liked the sort of book that hits you over the head, bangs in your ears, sucks the breath out of your lungs, and then blows it all right back in your face. You might say he was made to order (à la carte) for French food books.

One day he sat in a two-star Parisian restaurant, eating a full serving of Curds et Whey Almondine, a Norman special in which two curds and one whey are stuffed into the same almond and left for dead. He kept thinking about publishing this book as his all–time triumph. He thought of the Croix d'Or he could get from the President of France. He thought of the publicity he could get as a man of many tongues. He dreamed of the profits, which he could use to set up the greatest French Food in the World Museum and show how French cooking, having started in a small restaurant in 15ᵗʰ –century Venice, reached its glory when Louis XVII, served up as a Lemon Custard Trifle during one of the famous Masked Royal Balls, was promptly eaten.

As he sat there, overeating, he worried. Could it not be a presumption for him to publish such a book? Would people laugh at him too soon behind their hands? Could he publish this book and still hang on to the things that counted most to him, his pride in his country bread, his love for his American passport photo, and the honor of his latest alternative minimum tax payment?

As he ate and ate, and drank and drank, there came that special moment of enlightenment Cicero used to call "In vino lux."[2] It struck him that if he were to combine the surprises of French food with some even greater surprises too wild and daring ever to have been tried before, he would probably find the GFFB in the W the biggest seller on both the non-fiction and fiction lists. Suddenly, another "In Vino Lux" came. The greater surprise would be this: an American author.

The more he thought of it, the more delighted he became. He could feel the shock waves that would radiate out from France when this book hit the stalls along the banks of the Seine. He could hear the oratory in the Chambre des Députés. He could see the headlines in *Le Figaro*. He could see the heads bowed in grieved silence outside the now-shuttered windows of Restaurant Lapérouse. He could see the President of France officially creating a second eternal flame, directly beneath the emptied pots at *Hercule.*

Thrilled to think that he alone would publish a French food book designed to hold hungry Americans spellbound in a language all their own, the publisher immediately booked passage on a German-born jet and flew back home to find himself a suitable author.

By now you must be wondering whether his judgment was sound. Perhaps you are even saying to yourself that this book would already have been written if a felt need for it did in fact exist. Naturally, there is no easy answer to this. But one possible explanation is that felt needs are not always filled, even in the United States, no matter how well felt.

Another explanation is the possibility that the need was filled before it was well felt, and fulfillment was felt to be an anti-climax. (For as the saying goes, the filled and the felt soon

---

2 Literally, "Don't ever buy wine unless the light's on."

climax). But if the felt need were felt and filled, and in that order, and still no book had appeared, then there would be no ready explanation at all, and we would be caught on the horns of a dilemma. We would be left with no alternative but to steal a few recipes right out of French cuisine and solve the dilemma by cooking them emotionally.

A phenomenon like that takes a lot of explaining, and the author had great misgivings when he was first approached to do the book. Having hoarded all of his expertise throughout his life, which is both the prerogative of the expert and his only justification, he was reluctant to commit that expertise to print, lest he lose it there. It had seemed to him all along that the only good reason for doing The Greatest French Food Book in the World would be to further some worthy humanitarian cause like The Brotherhood of Food, and he was not sufficiently persuaded. As he told his friends, "Twenty three cents and The Brotherhood of Food will buy you a cup of bad coffee."

Clearly, then, something quite persuasive must have happened to our beloved author to force him into print, and we will keep you guessing no longer. It happened like this. The publisher was very nervous about going to his house and hitting him cold with the idea. He knew that a food expert is a tough nut to crack, since he feeds upon the fierce passions for food and drink that come of eating and drinking. He knew the French food expert in general and the American French food expert in particular. But the publisher finally decided that he had no other choice, since there are only twelve authentic French food experts in the whole world, and eight of them are politically to the left of Alec Baldwin.

So, with the same heave of courage that Maxime Duchesne used in Perth Amboy to create the DeLuxe Edition of *gâteau mouche aux fruits farcis* (in which a whipped lemon sourdough cake is slowly inflated with a filling of ground trout baked in herring and blown through a straw) the publisher went alone to the author's home. He found him in the kitchen. There was something so compelling about the unforgettable odors there that the publisher's nerves got the best of him, and before he could explain the purpose of his mission, he fainted dead away into the author's prized petit cassoulet.

This was the same petit cassoulet that had been simmering on the author's back burner since his great-grandfather's death in 1864.[3] It will remain the readers' responsibility to judge the food worthiness of a food book publisher who plunges uninvited into the ancient and venerable cassoulet of a total stranger. The author himself was mercifully prepared for any food emergency. Noticing that the publisher's plunge had not broken the foil, he carefully lifted the besotted man's head off the cassoulet with a pair of tongs, put the lid back on the *cassoulet*, and temporarily decreased the flame from a mediocre low to a simmer in order to insure a steady simm.

It will console the reader to know that the publisher did not perish in the cassoulet; he thus left intact the precedent set by the author's great-grandfather. He was, however, suitably embarrassed, and withdrew to a nearby country inn, where over a period of days he nursed his simmered face back to its original flush. As he nursed himself, and thought about the incident, he found that it only whetted his appetite for the book.

Of course, he was reluctant to return to the author's home alone, lest the ancient and tantalizing cassoulet taboo smite him another good one with its flat-sided tongue. He wondered whether there would be better persuasion in numbers.

The more he thought about it, the more it seemed like the best solution. He knew, for example, that it was statistically

---

3 In contrast to the grand cassoulet, which simmers in a large stock pot, the petit cassoulet traditionally simmers in a 3" ramekin or in a double egg on the half shell.

improbable that a group of three or four food book publishers would all fall into the author's cassoulet, and almost certainly not at the same time. But then he remembered the old American saying, too many cooks spoil the broth, and he lapsed again into uncertainty. He doubted whether there was any chance he might be lucky enough to find the author back at his cassoulet, where heat and bubbling aromas might soothe him into acquiescence.

He looked at himself in the mirror, a short, plump man, suitable for roasting, and it suddenly struck him. He was a publisher, and what he needed most was the elevation of authority. Putting on a "toque blanche" done in silk at Givenchy, and calling together three other and taller publishers, they devised a plan and then set out for the author's home.

It was almost five o'clock the following afternoon when they arrived. They were told that the author was still at lunch. With shrinking enthusiasm, they cooled their heels in the solarium until exactly twenty two minutes past five, or just after the entrée, whichever came first. Then they were summoned. Suddenly their very high spirits gave way and they broke into erratic flatulence. They looked at each other with hopeless aspiration. They sighed a heavy sigh. Finally, however, they called upon their courage and with the kind of awkward reverence one expects of a nun who has suddenly and unaccountably found herself in the warm-up room at the local YMCA, they entered the author's presence.

Keeping their eyes lowered so as to get used to the brilliant light, they got down on their stomachs in the time-honored tradition of those who employ experts. Their hands were heavy with petition, their eyes glazed with an honest profit motive, their wallets aching with hunger. Addressing him entirely from the horizontal, the publishers acknowledged that they had come to talk food.

From the author, there was a long and languid silence, followed by a lightly flavored but not entirely abruptive belch. Accepting this as a go-ahead, the publishers told him that they had come to try to persuade him to write The Greatest French Book in the World. This so intrigued the author that he picked up his wine.

Noting the excited flush on his glass, the publishers took heart. They rushed on to explain that the great novelty of the enterprise, and the thing that would excite the continent of Europe to such a degree that more than one clod was sure to be washed away from the continent, was the utterly simple, utterly incredible fact that the book was to be done by an American.

When the author heard this, his mouth suddenly went agape with a gape so cavernous that the publishers even from the horizontal could see the down on his whistle. However, as they were unaccustomed to the symmetry of his gapes, they were unable to tell whether his was the gape that refreshes or the gape that kills, so they held their breath for as long as the author held his gape.

When his gape began to decline, their countenances visibly brightened. They told him how they had hired a bevy of market research analysts and public opinion pollsters and instructed them to use all the available scientific processes of the modern imagination to find out whether the United States did indeed need a French food book.

These hired worthies had talked with and polled representative groups of American French food novices in every state of the union, on selected Indian reservations, and even on an island territory, which had made itself available in exchange for greater Franco-American spaghetti.

What these pollsters and analysts reported back was that they had heard rising up from thousands and thousands of French food novices all across the land a great hue and cry, though most especially a hue: "Give us a book that carries us beyond the humdrum world of Stillborn Toadstools in Aspic, or Caterpillar Kidneys Wounded by White Wine, into a more real world. Help us to learn the French people, and, in the learning, come to love them. Only then will we really be able to understand their food. But that won't prevent us from cooking it."

The author was so struck by this that he put his wine glass down right into the middle of his *Feuilles du Tabac Braisées au jus* (Braised Tobacco Leaves, in the original juice.) Having thus accommodated his wine in the grand manner,[4] he listened very intently by holding his fork to his ear. Realizing that they had finally gained his attention, the publishers rushed on to explain that their scientists had learned something even more wondrous.

They had learned that the average American French food novice is not in search of such traditional French food rewards as the *Toque Soufflé*, the stained apron, the antique omelet pan with the original egg markings intact and initialed, or even the sort of technical razzle dazzle usually associated with French food (the kind in which one learns to poach a bass in salad dressing while the salad itself is being eaten.) No, they learned that the American French food novice wants not so much to have an affair with French food as to marry it.

Even a boor would have to admit that it was the sort of affecting scene that fans of Harry Potter would have drenched their handkerchiefs over. The author believes that this deserves to be recorded as one of the truly illuminated pages in the annals of food history. Here were four grown men, rich and well-known

---

4 Viniculteurs (winebathers) are said to be able to predict the exact moment of orgasm by the balance between the tobacco juice itself, the voice of the grape, and the position of Mars in the Big Dipper.

pillars of the industry, men of uncertain nationality, who were so eager to lift French food out of its doldrums that they were willing to prostrate themselves at the feet of an American French food expert and beg him for mercy.

Inspired by the obvious humanitarianism in their character, and excited by the results of the market research, the author finally grasped the full significance of their visit. They were trying to tell him that he had in his own American backyard the greatest French food novitiate in the world. He suddenly saw himself as novice master to millions of American tongues. Then and there he decided that, no matter how large the profits to himself, he would accept the publisher's plea and go into print.

And so did it come to pass that he fashioned this book from whole cloth. The first printing, in the high dozens, met great critical success. "Here at last," said the reviewers, "is the authoritative and the definitive. Here in one book is the authentic and the virtual. The American French Food novice has finally been irradiated."

IV

How to Read this Book

As you probably suspect by now, this is a read-it-yourself book. It is written in the language of instruction, and should offer difficulty only to readers whose language is other than their own. One of the characteristics that help make this book unique among the French food books of our time is in fact its willingness to be read.

There are several *'caveat lectors'* to be issued right away. The first is that this book can be read either aloud or silently, but never both, at least not simultaneously. If it is being read aloud, the reader should take care to allow a pause for breath first prior to, and immediately after, all parentheses and italics, no matter what language they are in.

If, on the other hand, it is being read silently, and there is a word or phrase from original French that refers to some kind or suggestion of food, it is customary to salivate heavily right to the end of the sentence. (If it is a question, or interrogative sentence, this means no one is sure of the French, and you need not salivate at all).

Salivation is never done when the book is being read aloud, as it interrupts the rhythm of the page and draws attention to the water spots on the front of your clothes, which, if the sentence is long enough, will mildew. If it is being read aloud, it is also customary to emphasize the names of famous foods and their creators with a deep, but brief, genuflection. This requires the reader to remain standing whenever reading the book aloud, unless you are fairly accomplished at the art of genuflecting while seated.

This book has also been designed for people who want to read it aloud, whether they are reading it to themselves or to someone else. Furthermore, the structure and language of the book have been created in such a way that the book actually allows and even invites more than one person to read it aloud simultaneously (unless one of them wishes to remain silent.) The possibilities are therefore almost limited.

A single reader can read it aloud to self, to another, or to others, -whether or not the another or the others are reading it aloud. If the others are reading it aloud, they can read it aloud separately as well as together, but are not required to read it aloud to another or to each other, even though they may read it aloud in each other's presence, whether or not they are in the same room.

If another is reading it aloud to other than the reader, the other can be in the same room or in a different room than either the reader or the another, and if there are more than one, the others may be read to at the same time or at different times, wherever they are. But if others are reading it aloud to another, and the another is not in the same room or at the same time, then it will have to be read even more loudly than when the reader is reading the book aloud to others who are not in the same room at the same time, and are not reading it simultaneously.

A few other hints on reading will help you get through the book with a vision of sugarplums still pirouetting in your head. If the book is to be read silently, by you or by anyone else, the nature of the silence will depend on whether it is being read silently by a single reader who is alone, or by a single reader who is in the presence of others, or by more than one reader who are alone, or by more than one reader who are in the presence of others, or by a single reader who is in the presence of others who are not themselves reading this book, or by more than one reader who are in the presence of others who are, or are not, reading this book.

Essentially, the distinction between the most appropriate silences while reading this book is a simple one, and it calls for a simplistic mind. In the first, second and fourth instances, the silence that will work most effectively is the single silence, characterized by pursed lips, a low but vibrant humming, and open vowels. In the third, fifth and sixth instances, the multiple silence will work best. It is characterized by several pairs of pursed lips, a low but vibrant chorus of hums, and distinguished dental work. In either case, the silent reader(s) will find that although all diphthongs in the book are edible, the consonants are only mildly so.

V

Brief Opening Remarks

A lot of people who have been caught lunching in the garden at *Les Particulières* during a rainstorm are all wet when they say that in France everybody talks about the weather but nobody does anything about the food. It is as easy for the French to resist doing something about their food as it is for Lily Tomlin to resist broadcasting the Yankee games. For it is an ill-disputed fact that food eats its way into French life to such an extent that French life often eats its way back into the food.

Nor is this a new phenomenon, much as we might wish it were, since old phenomena have a kind of familiarity that breeds contempt. The congruence of life and food is one of those straightforward facts the French will bend over backward to provide you, leaning over fancies on their way, and no one is going to gainsay an old phenomenon like that, least of all this book.

French cuisine has become so popular in France that it is often eaten there. This might come as a surprise to people who have not eaten in France, but it will come as a double surprise to those who have. It is the contention of this book, therefore, that not everyone can make that statement. But it is also the contention of this book that, if they could, they would, since it is a perennial of human nature to make contentions, no matter how apt, and this book is no exception.

If it were an exception, it could no longer be the rule, and this is not the time for any book to try being an exception when it has not even been the rule, particularly since it is a book of contentions in an age when contentions are king. Anyone who is emotionally incapable of sustaining contentions is advised to stop here, at least for a short rest, before going on to the similarly exciting and improvident contentions with which the rest of the book could well do without.

When the announcement was first made that the French had gotten a step closer to their food, they were miffed. Why hadn't they been told? they asked. Why had they been kept in the dark? But it was their *food* that had been kept in the dark, and they were told that the only way to avoid being kept in the dark in the future was to keep their mouths open.

In spite of their miff, the important message reaching the outside world was that the French and their food had reached a new plateau in their ever-ascending progress towards a complete *entente cordiale*, and it is the very bone of this book's most envied contentions that we must not leave it up to the French to explain this phenomenon, for fear they may be able to.

A book such as this, which proposes to add the stature of scholarship and the throes of glaucoma to a subject that is ordinarily limited by the four walls of a kitchen, may well deserve the reader's divided attention, but it would be foolish to stop there. People who get up early enough to be able to read this book without being outlawed by Food and Drug Act agents deserve at the outset the luxury of a few definitions, and above all a satisfying definition of French cuisine guaranteed to add still another measure of marrow to the bone of this book's most prized contentions.

The results of a recent poll taken throughout France by hand, so that it would not get lost in the shuffle, have been published in *Mechanics Illustrated* as another long series of attempts by Unesco to improve international misunderstanding. The results show that, as of the end of the final meal of the eating year, a full six percent of all French food qualified as cuisine. As soon as France read all about it on the Foods Anonymous page of *Artificial Food Additives of Southwest France*, there rose across the land a hue and a cry, though most specially this time a cry. What, they wanted to know, was all the rest of the food, and where was it?

Further statistics were charted, graphs were consulted, highways were scoured, plates were cleaned, and then came the answers. Except for the six percent that was cuisine, the rest was food. Furthermore, over seventeen percent of the total food in average daily attendance throughout France that day was eaten by the French themselves. Twenty four percent was eaten by Eastern European refugees and other recondites anxious for a hot meal.

The remaining thirty-one percent was exported to developed nations under a profit-making grant from the Ford Foundation. Numericals who expect these percentages to total one hundred percent, and others equally supple of finger, will conclude that the French must either improve their arithmetic or eat faster. In any case, it becomes increasingly possible that when an American tries to talk about the French and their food, he finds himself at a loss for food.

VI

Food Happy

Litterbugs of French history only have to go back as far as Chateaubriand to show that a dry historical truth can still be a lot of laughs. Chateaubriand was the first French grandee to try to chronicle the developing relationships between the French and their food. In a lavish of introspection, Chateaubriand was the first to describe that relationship as complicated as the Snow White and Seven Dwarfs gestalt. Dandet, the failed gourmet, unlike Chateaubriand in that he was just enough for one other person, agreed with him.

"The feeling between the average French person and food is as intimate and yet surprising as the hand of an ungloved hemorrhoidist," said Dandet. But perhaps the last word came just last night from the Veterans of French Territorial Expansions, Unltd., who gathered at Fontainebleau to debate from memory the development of the international French food market. These wise and able longevities came to the climactic conclusion that the love of France for food is more conspicuous than the clitoris of Rosie O'Donnell.

Such bouquets as these are enough to take the rust off the plumbing on the Eiffel Tower, but, lest the misled go astray, it is also necessary to add early in this book that French food has its defectors. When a French food defector is hiding amidst the forest green, his nose cocked, his buttons open, and harking with every bit of hark at his command to the declines of French food, he still cannot resist defecting as gently as he can. A French food defector is not, therefore, the insultor that many take him to be. He puts it mildly so that no one's taste buds will fail to bloom.

Nevertheless, he is also a sincere, and it is only with the greatest conviction that he and his fellow defectors say they do not care whether the French movie star Gerard Depardieu traversed the exploits of schizophrenia and the temptations of curiosity when he refused to identify the co-author of his autobiography. They say they find French food amiss, and no matter how bizarre the fringes of French culture, at heart the whole culture is sick of food, for nothing good can be said of a national sovereignty that inspires questions as retrograde as "Does France imitate food, or does food imitate France? And if so, why not?"

French food defenders answer thus: Intelligent questions like these, challenging though they may be, can only be fully comprehended when compared with equivalent national questions from other sovereignties. Take as one sample the national question of the United States, and it will lift you off your feet in proof positive that some countries can use some proof positive. In the United States the streets and barbershops shelter millions of bewildered citizens asking each other askance, "If life is really an imitation of art, can I get it at a discount?"

This is the sort of question that could send fleeing back to the pits any citizen only recently denatured by alcohol, but it at least demonstrates one important characteristic. Whereas food is central to the national questions of France, the American question proves there is only limited nutritional value in quotation marks.

A nation in love with food is a happy nation. We know that, and as the ancient proverbs tell us, Happiness is next to cleanliness, except in France, where cleanliness supersedes godliness. What is more, happiness makes the heart grow fonder, and since happiness is as happiness does, the French do something. This book is the first to reveal what they do. They let a smile be their umbrella, and then they sit down to lunch beneath.

Perhaps all their sunshine is due to the fact that the French know the way to a man's stomach is through his esophagus, and so in a nation that eats happy it is fitting that the first sign of spring be a tan on the back of the throat. There is, however, no magic in their happiness. They simply follow one or two basic rules of thumb, the first of which is *"Une hirondelle ne fait pas le printemps."*

As every reader knows, the meaning of this famous cliché is pastoral: "One swallow does not make a summer." But in this case, the cliché translates quite handily, "One swallow does not make an alcoholic," – the sort of thing that inspires the traditional French *fiancée* to urge her beloved, "Drink to me only with thine eyes."

Another rule of thumb long since enthroned as a commandment first came down from Ararat on a raft of chickory surrounded by tablets clearly graven with images that spelled 'Prilosec.' The commandment, now known to be Number Two of ten, is "Know thy fodder as thyself." For centuries it was taken as nothing more than a shenanigan, until Alistair Choufleur, the only male member of the staff at *La Toque Blanche* to stuff ganders entirely on the horizontal, urged it very seriously upon the encyclopaedists when he gave up the gloves of office upon retiring from his position.

With suitable nationwide advertising, the encyclopaedists managed to persuade the nation that this was as suitable a commandment for serious French consumption as the unequivocal "It's a long way to Tipperary" is suitable for Ireland. If any commandment is a good commandment, they said, how much the better is the food commandment! They were right. A well-said food commandment helps both the French, and those born in some corner of a foreign field that is forever tourist, to guide their stomach's happiness.

The first sight of French food happiness is not always the clearest, because to be food happy is not necessarily to look food happy. On the contrary, food happiness can wear a most disagreeable face, sometimes making the French look like their livers have permanently stewed in piss and cabbages. But as you get to know them, it becomes increasingly obvious that their hearts are really wreathed in strawberry aspic, and on the closest inspection you find a little bit of love and a little bite of food coexisting happily on the lips, on the laps, and on the lungs of every citizen in France.

You have only to ask one of them about happiness, and the reply is instant food: "Of course I am happy! Didn't you see the sparrow marmalade I made last spring? Not only that, but it was right in this garden, – over there by the stuffed olives – that Robert Browning composed that poem of his... how did it start?... Yes. I remember:

> I send my heart up to thee,
> all my heart. In this my singing...

Heady stuff, right? Well, nobody but me knows who he wrote it to. It was to one of my grandfather's prize rutabagas." Alas, say the French, the Americans do not share our view of life through a casserole. Ask an American about happiness, and there is no mention of food: "Of course, what do you mean, happy! My linoleum shine lasted three commercials longer than yours did, right? And look at my car. It has much bigger breasts than yours does!"

French love for food has made the history of France unique, in that it is littered with the carcasses of food martyrs. Many history books, like Germaine's *"Alcoholic Uses of Linseed Oil in Toulouse-Lautrec, 1849-1885."* attest to the fact that, just as organized religions have subcommittees on sacrifice, martyrdom is the *summa cum laude* of the food faithful.

And just as there are varieties of incest, there are variations in martyrdom. There is the wholesale national sacrifice, as in the case of Cuba, which is currently sacrificing all personal comfort and social security as an integral part of its fifty-year plan to transfer the entire island onto the mainland of Florida.

But by far the worthiest sacrifice, so say the French, is the highly stylized, individual food immolation. This is the kind that really proves every ecstasy has its agony. One of the most touching agonies is memorialized by a small statue in the square of a drab French village called Centre de Merde:

Thomas Beaulieu de Fain
Died April 18, 1949
In Defense of his Coquilles St. Jacques

When people like Beaulieu de Fain make themselves sacrificial lambs on the altar of culinary arts, the French believe it proves they care more about food than any people on earth, – a braggadocio that reminds us that Nehru once said, "Comparisons are as odious as a bath in the Ganges." But once and for all it settles the question of who loves food the most, for it is virtually impossible to imagine anyone but a Frenchman announcing to a firing squad: "I could not love my death so much, loved I not Squab Supreme."

But martyrdom is only one piece of the evidence that in France food occupies a place larger than an underdeveloped country's dream of having Rockefeller Center as its very own colony. Still another proof is the subtlety of French food, and the *éclair* is the perfect illustration. Just as one goes to Bolivia for some deep breaths of political congestion, or to Beijing for a look at the emperor's clothes, one goes to France for the subtlety of an *éclair*, even though many foreigners think of the *éclair* as a flimsy and a parvenu.

The reason for its subtlety is that the French consider the *éclair* an elemental force. If it has an accent *aigu* (´), they say, then you must eat it from front to back, but if the accent is *grave* (`) then the situation is serious and you must take another look at it, which, in the avuncular of French diplomacy, means you should eat it backwards.

So it is not easy to deflate the fact that the French consider all other nations mere pretenders to the food throne they think they occupy. The Tastevins de Omaha tried to claim a little latitude for the greatness of American cuisine by pointing out that the French national folk hero, the croissant, has as great a percentage of air as the American folk hero, the hamburger, has fat.

This only excited the French defenders to point out that the national anthem of France, the rollicking *Bouillabaisse*, is much more zestful and every bit more tasteful than its American counterpoint, the Jelly Roll Blues. In short, they want no mistake made about it. They demand to be acknowledged as superior at the stove and, - everymuch as important, - in the refrigerator.

One way to treat a French citizen who is pinning a fourth star on the national glottis is to pooh-pooh the whole idea of food superiority. The French are known to have a deep-throated aversion to the pooh, and particularly to transatlantic poohs, so incoming transatlantic poohs are very heavily taxed in accordance with French customs, although all outgoing poohs are sent free of charge.

The point is that one may pooh, and one may pooh-pooh, but it is not always a question of whether one poohs, or where. Rather, it is a question of which pooh one uses to pooh-pooh the French glottis. In concert with the spirit of that time-honored saying, "Whistle the pooh," the true pooher can only produce a very translatable version when standing fully clothed outside the windows of Air France. After all, it matters not if one moos the pooh, whinnies the pooh, or crows the pooh, it is a pooh nonetheless, and the French know a pooh when they smell one.

Contrarily, there is always the counter-pooh. The fact is that French food tastes so much that the French use this fact to prove that, if they are not the world's best cooks, they certainly cook the world's best food. This is not simply due to the love of ostentation that has ever bedeviled French penury, but to the fact that, when given the choice, the French take the low-option family plan. They are traditionally as low-key as a ballade for bassoon and bass.

Hamlet himself once called the French as melancholic as an afternoon in the Fossils room at the Benevolent and Protective Order of Elks. Because of these characteristics, cooking can now be understood as the most effective way for the French to keep their spirits up, and this further explains why the unmitigated pooh can play such havoc with the nation's self-esteem, for the French believe that great food not only enlivens their tertiary glands, but opens their legs wider.

Hugues Verlaine, the iconoclast who was forced to dump his icons onto the antiques market when his vowels gave out, once explained this to an audience of laughers brought into a studio at Mont St. Michel in order to tape them at their loudest for use at the next English coronation. Our culinary successes used to repel the invader, he said, but now they invade the repellent, because we French have a quality of character that is deeply in-baked, and looks like a pound cake on its way to a slenderella salon.

He then drove home his point with a thump heard round the rib cage. "To test whether the French are done," he warned, "prod them in the middle. If they spring back at you, they are completely done." As you might expect, the French attribute this resiliency to the power of their food, for when they are down and out, they lift up their heads and shout, "It's going to be a great meal."

VII

What Price Victory?

Of all the people that eat upon this globe, none is as anxious as the French to view their foods as *objets d'art*. When they announce that it is going to be a great meal, the real query soon becomes, "Exactly how great?" There are so many ways to calculate. The easiest is to consult any recent edition of the well-nigh Guide Michelin, France's most prestigious index of tire dealers, which will also show that one out of every three Frenchmen will have eaten at a two-star restaurant at least once before she dies, and often on the very day.

It notes further that one out of every two Frenchwomen will have eaten at a three-star restaurant four times in her life for five hours each at an average cost of ninety euros per meal, but for all Frenchmen who have been waiters at a four-star restaurant for a minimum of three weeks, two great chefs will have been born once a year. These figures tend not only to aggravate the zest in French cuisine; they also disprove de Maupassant's theorem that the sum of French culinary arts is equal to a portrait in the basement of the Louvre.

The second easiest way to calculate the value of French food is to ask the average American, whose spiritual zenith crests at the height of a Wendy's Baconator, whether statistics will prove the pudding. On the basis of extensive research done by the White House's Office of Management and Budget, we now know that the average American resists statistics with the same passion a congressman resists a photo of himself on the front page of the New York Times.

But statistics themselves do not necessarily prove anything more about French food than is already suspected, so all average Americans, and those who read this book, are advised to approach statistical evidence with the same jaundiced eye the former Governor of South Carolina used to reserve for a fragile condom.

If, after all, statistics were all that conclusive, the law of probability would have determined that one of the three Magi would have been both French and female, and, better still, would have declared frankincense and myrrh *trivia non grata*, and brought the child something to eat instead.

The only real rule for evaluating the worth of French food was inaugurated at the Académie Culinaire in Cardin-les-deux-Ciseaux. Called the Golden Rule, it suggests that one pursue the dividend by dividing the seasons into four-quarter time, and while multiplying all the loaves by half the fishes, reduce the French social contract by the perimeter of a square meal. The French, at least, find it fun; Americans find it mathematics.

Yet the French are understandably inimical to the idea that an outlander even wants to evaluate the worth of their food. They tend to consider such an effort as the sort of thing one comes to expect from such loonies as the harpist who plays "Jesus On Thy Lap Abiding" at a Bar Mitzvah.

The French have long maintained that anyone who needs arithmetic to evaluate food is a woebegone, because by retreating to numbers he admits he has lost confidence in his mouth, – just as William Jennings Bryant must have done when he found himself strangling on the Cross of Gold. Scorned and abused, the food calculator will be told that, if measure he must, let him parade through a ten-course dinner with a tape measure on his gout.

But when all is said and eaten, it really *is* possible to compute the value of French food via an arithmetic exercise which, when coupled with some minor byplay on the abacus, can produce protein results. The secret is in noting that the zero on the abacus is as concave as it is convex, and is thus in the enviable position of being able to see both sides of the meal.

Taking the zero for what it is, a past minus but a future plus, the evaluator need only be reminded that he who looks ahead had better keep an eye on his malice aforethoughts, lest the oven cool. For those who are no strangers to numbers but some strangers to Chinese, an abacus is best described as worry beads elevated to technology. The beads have been put on horizontal wires in order to increase the speed with which a person can worry, particularly since vertical wires would let the beads slip to the bottom and fall asleep.

The abacus is especially useful to the Chinese in that it helps them be far more accurate in counting their worries, for in the Chinese culture it is not as important to rid yourself of worries as to be able to say with mathematical certainty just how many worries you have. The French, on the other hand, never worry when they are on the horizontal. They call the abacus "beads on a roost," in recognition that you need not worry that a bead sitting with a wire through its middle will ever rule, however it roosts. One must infer, on the other hand, that if you are worried about French food, you are the perfect candidate for an abacus.

Let us assume for the sake of the abacus that you are about to calculate the value of a 4 by 9 inch platter of Sea Urchins Beauregard in accordance with Lord's Rule of the Roost. In this cleanest of all the abacus foreplays, the beads are colored white, black, red and yellow in accordance with the intensity of the worry, with white representing the least, or minor, worry.

Starting with the color of the sea urchins in question, which can be an acne red but are often horde yellow, you move the appropriate bead one worry each until you have devised a worry in triplicate. The progression proceeds from there by adding one worry at a time, and following each even worry with an odd worry so as to put to rights any worries that are temporarily uneven, or a little ill at ease.

When the color of the sea urchins and the depth of the platter are matched by the additional burden you feel, count the beads on the top row only, until you have covered the length of the platter, and then divide by the number of sea urchins. The resulting worry is then colored by number, at which point the number on the roost represents not only the value of the food, but the week's calorie count for a pride of World Wrestling Entertainers.

It was this same geometric that San Savarin used to offset the conclusion that Cherries on the Half Pit were worth only half their weight of old. If this exercise proves resistant, either grease the wires, or change your tune completely and compute the value of a Compote of Salamander, which is always a puce green, and thus double the worry.

If one is to believe the prefaces to the great French cookbooks or the Letters to the Editor in *Woman's Day*, French cuisine is the alter ego of French food. Although a portion of Larded Pine Needles in Resolved Leechee Nuts tastes and looks exactly the way it sounds, it is widely believed that when the same portion is served in France, it looks like a celebration cake and tastes like lobster Newburg.

For the person who remains confused about what cuisine really is, unable to tell at what point the addition of fresh pepper, a bouquet of seasonings, and two lardons elevates a veal stew into an international shrine, the easiest rule of tongue is this: If the title of the entrée has three or more words, it is quite possibly cuisine. If the entrée comes on two or more plates, it is quite probably cuisine. If it costs more than 74 euros, it *is* cuisine.

French economists can now state without fear of impunity that the increased popularity of French cuisine is at least partially attributable to the growing fact that a number of Frenchmen can afford it. It used to be true that the everyday French child was brought up to believe that the cashier in a cuisine-centered restaurant was a part-time boatman over the River Styx, for there was a time when they could only afford to eat on the Marshall Plan, and they were only allowed one of the midget appetizers or the salad, and then had to hang around nearby tables embezzling seltzer water, and hoping the American Express Travelers Checker would accidentally drop the anchovy filet off his Combination Plate.

The French now claim they can afford their own cuisine because their spirits are expanding far enough to cover the check, though most waiters would protest that the French fist has never yet grown beyond the circumference of a euro. Whatever the reason, the popularity of food is the opposite of a charley horse, and might explain why last year twelve percent more French citizens entered French restaurants than left them.

Popular though it may be, French cuisine is still unforgettably expensive, whether on foreign or domestic soil. Indeed, the memory of French restaurant prices still burns a hole in the minds of all those budget-minded tourists who have had to decide every day, in the privacy of their trenches along the Boul' Matisse, whether to spend their day's budget on a twenty-minute stretch aboard a lovable French spreadeagle, or blow it all on the typical sixty-euro (appx. $84) meal featuring a semi-tasse of *espresso* concentrate and two demi-buttered brioches.

This kind of blind-man's choice may explain why a not-unpopular American image of continuous foreign aid is the large French family still living handsomely on the profit made way back in the World War from selling bareheaded doughboys a fifteen-franc family lunch featuring a dab of mutton grits and several thickset carrots with greens atop.

One can also hint at the expense of French cuisine by noting the tone of reunions among tourists returned from France: The middle-aged female atheist from Racine, upon meeting her old boon, the hopeful gonorrheac from Wichita, remembers her only in one dimension: "Say, weren't you the one that had those 77-euro sauteed squirrel breasts with me in Toulon last June?" The trendy monastic from Indiana, urinal to urinal with the gaping date retrievalist from IBM, has his memory juggled thus: "The 104-euro entrée at La Coupole? The 104-euro entrée? (Gasp) Oh, my God, the 104-euro entrée! When did you get back?"

Inflated prices may not be any more of the rule than they are of the exception, except when overinflated, but sensible tourists on the loose in France tend to remember their hotel by counting their change, and return to their native climes remembering the Saint Chapelle not by the name or sight, but by its propinquity to Chez Putaine, where they had to shell out 49 euros per serving for a Prawn Tart with whipped cream and no water.

Such economic incidents may be an insult to French cooking, but they are eloquent testament to the French knack for getting a foreigner to put her money where her mouth is. When another planeload of American tourists bedecks at Philadelphia, clutching receipts from a week of French restaurants, chefs in Paris may weep with relief, but the French economy prospers, though no tourist can truthfully say he is the richer for it, except around the waist.

VIII

Tween Tongue and Cheek

Even the woeful Shriner knows by now that to understand French cuisine is to overprice it. Yet no one knows why, not even the French themselves. Their refractors will apply all the usual hoary stereotypes, claiming that the French people are only cheap because they are inexpensive, and so they talk cheap and eat less. The secret of the cost of French cuisine is in the very ills of these illogics: its cost depends upon the French language, and French is the most expensive language in the world.

This little known but long remembered link between tongue and check shows that if language be the food of money, it is as expensive to cook a French recipe as to mispronounce it, and exorbitant to read the whole thing aloud, except at masses where Berlioz is the featured musicale.

Indeed, this may well account for the almost total silence in French supermarkets, a sort of reverential calm that rises toward worship between the executed salami and the New Zealand hare paste. It may also explain why the greatest sin in France is not to have a face more cryptic than Sarkozy's, but to allow a recipe to be translated into any other language, particularly a language understood by anyone else.

But all this may well be a lack-a-day-dee. The grammarians who syntax daily whether the most expensive French word of all is the dangling participant or the future perfect marsupial have identified the vital point of modern French cuisine: the French language is getting even more expensive.

French was not so expensive when it was younger, and it was far more universally popular on the diplomatic trunk circuit between 1800 and 1950 than any other language. This was due in large letters to two very basic facts. The first was that it was the only language in western and eastern Europe with which diplomats could elaborate their surrender negotiations so baroquely that by the time the terms of surrender were fixed, both nations had had a complete rest and a new coat of arms, and could resume their war affably.

The second, perhaps even the next, reason was that if you were in any embassy in the world during that period, and you were unable to speak French, you would starve. And if you tried to nimble your fingers at the cook to tell him that you needed food, he would either tell you in French to go jack your nimbles, or give you what modern pederasts call the finger foods. So it was that the connection between the preeminence of French food and the universal use of the French language seemed a strangle-hold not even Justin Bieber could break.

But by the turn of the century vexators knew that French food language was unduly addicted to punctuation, particularly to hypothetical punctuation, and so could not last forever. The number of those who were eating French food in order to improve their accent began to decrease. A store in Caracas began to sell cookbooks in English. Betty Crocker left Paris forever to return to her native stove outside Berlin. But it was in 1950 that the French food language finally went into parentheses and took low-cost food with it.

It happened that the Secretary-General of the United Nations had introduced the hamburger by popular resolution to the General Assembly, where it was an instant acclaimed and a total resolved. But when delegates and orderlies ordered a hamburger in French in New York City, it tasted as if it were high on the grease and low in the bun. Thenceforward hamburgers were ordered in American. It is said that, had these worthies been able to order a hamburger in French, perhaps the price of French food today would not instantly mummify the salivary glands.

The final blow to French as the *lingua franca* of food came in 1962, when the then J.B. Kennedy, later to gain international facsimile for making the most astounding archaelogical discovery of the century on an island not entirely off Greece, turned at a state dinner in honor of the Chateau de Chambord and asked her next-plate neighbor, an American oil duchess, to pass her a handful of Pacquin's. J.B. poignantly preferred the American pronunciation, "the Pak-winz," to the more gelatinous "Pah-can."

The whole state dinner almost fled its borders when they overheard her, for the French had long feared the day when all those rich American tourists might stop trying to prove that they could eat as much as or even more than they could tip, and turn instead to converting French food into the American language.

The prime nominee for heading such a campaign was any noticeable member of America's faux royalty, since by popular agreement, there is no faux royalty quite like American faux royalty, in that they are the only ones who really try to earn a crown. When the then J.B.K.O asked for her favorite cold-cream, Pacquin's, and in American, it was the long-awaited declaration that thenceforward Americans could talk French food.

The results of this *pronunciamento* were immediately obvious. The kitchen milkmaid, an unlikely by the name of Juliette L'Enfant, sensed that one effect would be a large new market for ready-to-wear food in the United States. So she quickly changed her name to Julia, translated her recipes into American, lengthened her dress, and tuned herself into a new job.

A second result was that the day after the dinner, the French language actually rose sixteen points on the New York Stock Exchange, bolstered as it was by the American dollar, and it has been going up ever since, taking the price of French food with it, especially in France, where it cannot be cooked in American. Any responsible broker will tell you that, as the French language goes up in price, it gets rarer, so whoever eats French food in France savors not only a little financial crisis, but also a bit of history, and none too soon.

IX

I Regret I Have but One Life to Give for my Recipes

Taking the French out of French food can be tantamount to taking the coals out of their mines, and, quite naturally, the French resist the pillage. They feel they have firmly established food as their exclusive province, especially after they lost Algeria and Vietnam, and they defend it with such an armada of food squelches that few dare to meet them on that greatest of all the Fields of Gold—the tablecloth.

Examples of the devastation are precocious. For instance, when an exonerated German frau visiting from Germany-am-Rhine happens to pride herself on the regal Venetian red of her garden tomatoes, her French hostess announces that *her* tomatoes are the same Verona red all the Paris galleries are showing, and, what is more, the exact red of the Doge's Palace that came through the dirt when the Louvre finally cleaned its Tiepolo.

If an American attacks with the notion that the French only drink wine to fuzz up their physiques so that others can more easily distinguish them from the French hairless, the French will counter that they are the ones who taught the Chinese that the best way to press duck is first to deflate it by acupuncture, and then go easy on the starch.

But the essence of the stranglehold the French try to hold over food is best exemplified by the words of Louis Pasteur, long recognized as one of most grata of the world's medical persona. When asked by the doughty Dagmar, Baroness Holstein-Angus, to explain how Germany could ever be blessed by French food, Pasteur replied that the truest test of a superlative French *pepperade* was its ability to produce a minor gesundheit.

The French are at their vivacious and bug-eyed best when they are in search of the eternal verities and are using food and drink as their medium. One comes across this very special quality in oddly amusing circumstances. When one awakes in a small hotel room near Salade-aux-Deux-Magots (a small church-inspired village 20 kilometers east of Deauville, noted for its staggering collection of pesticides) and hears through the wine-scattered wallpaper the morning conversation of a bridal couple, one realizes why France is first in food and first in the hearts of its countrymen.

It becomes clear from their conversation that they admire wine-scattered wallpaper for its own sake, not just because it tends to be self-standing, but because it usually represents a happy mix of vintage and table wines. A nation dotted with bridal couples intent on appreciating wine-scattered wallpaper as a prelude to breakfast reminds us that Lovelace, English though he was down to his uninflamed appendix, was not exactly poetic when he wrote of France: "Stone walls do not a prison make, nor iron bars a cage, but try wine-scattered wallpaper, and know true liberty."

The admiration of wines on a wine-scattered wallpaper is not always enough to furnish the conversational hitchhiking so vital to marital conjunction. Therefore, loving couples will usually turn from the wallpaper, their hair teased, their armpits deoxygenated, and moon at each other with fluted breath, philosophizing on the contribution food can make to the internal truths with the same pulverizing questions for which French philosophers have been given their just desserts.

"Chéri, what is more?" they will ask each other, and then, perhaps innocently, "Cheri, what does 'less' mean?" Anyone on the other side of the wallpaper may not overhear the answers, and may not even wish to, for fear of gagging, but the very fact that someone in western civilization is trying to deal seriously with the heritage of French philosophy, and doing it though the medium of food, is enough to sustain any sagging marriage vows, for in turning food into thought, the French alone have captured the real flavor of Western culture, and then some.

X

The Element of Chance

One is sorely tempted to be inspired by the reverential chit-chat of French bridal couples philosophizing on the harmony of food and thought. To keep one's perspective, however, it must go without saying that your average philosopher is simply an ordinary human being with a question mark stuck in his throat, while the French philosopher, no matter how well unknown, has in fact swallowed it. Both have this in common: as long as the questions keep coming, they leave their mark.

The difference is that France has managed to lodge its questions so skillfully in the national diet that every French citizen becomes a questioner and a doubter very early in life. It can be said here in this book, for the very first time, that uncertainty gives us all food for thought, but for the French it is a lifetime meal. To counteract this, and as a way to help them face their future with pluck, France has developed a way of cooking some of the serendipity out of life. We will call it cooking with clairvoyance.

It all started with Claire, Madame de Pompadour, a high-browed lady and a rotunda who occupied the knees, thighs, and most of the groin of the parallel Louis for the better part of the three times in twelve years he did a-wooing go. Claire wanted to be sure that she would be around when it came time to write her mémoires, and so, realizing that a tool in hand is the first step toward fixing any situation, she learned to dally with Louis' power so adroitly that he thought her the most permanent part of his entourage, and she never once feared either that he would lose his place or she her grip.

But, as Cardinal dePlinval once said, impotence makes the high-brows weaker, and suddenly Pompadour found herself slipping away from Louis. As the truant officer says, "Absence makes the road grow stiffer," but it did not work for Claire, and the more they were apart, the more worried she became.

She said to her ladies, "Come, we will serenade our Louis while life and voice shall last, then we'll pass and be forgotten with the rest." She did not believe that would happen, but it did. One day she found she had no state secrets left to distribute. It seemed the end of her. But Claire was a supple: she held onto life and limb by handing out state guesses instead.

Claire's capacity for sustaining her future by marketing her uncertainties appealed to the French, and they dubbed the idea 'clairvoyance'. Clearly, they were ripe for the idea, –Louis himself had said, "Nothing is as strong as an idea that has come into Claire." The French were already so susceptible to such natural fragilities as the annual wine and perfume crops that they had changed mother nature's official status to that of a distant and not instantly cuddled kleptomaniac.

Realizing that what they did not know could not hurt anyone else, and what they did know would never help anyone at all, the French took to clairvoyance as a football star takes to deodorant promotions, but with even greater seriousness than B.F. Skinner would, in a later century, proliferate his discovery that he was an atheist because his pigeons were incapable of the original in original sin.

Of course, Claire de Pompadour only started the trend. France has been blessed with a long line of kings whose personal attributes have gained them the company of such other dazzling notorieties as Louise de la Vallière. Louise was one of those lovelies who was clairvoyant by persuasion. She was not exactly addicted to crystal balls, but she was far-sighted enough to stare into the pair entrusted to her care and thereby view firsthand the rise of the house of Bourbon, thus to predict whether anything would come of it, and also to see in those historic globes whether any other ladies were waiting offstage, as anxious as she to mount the throne.

Louise, in fact, had a double advantage. She knew how to cook. And so, building on de Pompadour's genius, she taught the French nation that if language be the food of love, they could cook themselves up a lot of romantic history. And they have.

XI

Through the Food-Glass Lightly

I t is said that a Frenchman and his food are seldom parted for longer than it takes to salt a pair of Rhinoceros Beetles Parmesan. This is another way of saying that a Frenchman and his food are seldom parted for more than the distance of a preposition. So it is understandable that French is a language almost entirely circumscribed by food, and seldom visible through it. As just one political example, there is a notable difference in an American and a French description of a union leader.

Americans prefer the physique to the food, and will describe any given union leader as a dedicated workaholic, or as a pain in the butt, or as a spherebuster. If they are Republicans, they might even observe that 69 divided by 3 equals 23 union leaders. The French, on the other hand, will describe the union leader by the contents of his backyard garden, by the names of his favorite restaurants, by the pet names for all his fish, and by the cooking competitions he has entered.

In any event, comparisons with food or descriptors related to food very rarely arise in the United States. French citizens, taking the at-large on the other side of their mouths, will prefer the more savory approach of describing one of their union leaders quite specifically as being as brittle as uncooked antlers, or as a perspirant who can successfully outpour the lugubrious pig, or as a man seasoned with a face of paprika and a voice of curry.

In effect, their language leads the French around by the nose and by their taste buds. In World War II they described Roosevelt so aromatically ("as spoiled as a Strasbourg goose") that one felt they had forgiven him his adenoids. And today their similes are as flavorful as they are historic: they say that every elevator passenger at Cartier is as coddled as eggs Rothschild.

The French even go a word further, and refer to other languages in terms of their own tastebuds. Portuguese reminds them of eggplant roe; Chinese is said to have the delicacy of a soufflé of candied minnows; and Arabic has the lungs of the great horny toad tossed in the style of Montand. With food ever on their lips, as well as in their mouths, the French have justified themselves as the salivants of the Western world.

It follows as pepper the salt that whereas the best Oxford English is heard in the lavatories of the Commonwealth, and the best American in the stadium bleachers, the best French is heard in the kitchen. Berlitz herself has never been able to improve upon the French lessons all Paris receives daily just from standing at the exhaust fan outside the kitchen of the Académie Française. One must conclude that if food be the love of language in France, then food must be the language of love.

After all, food is to national identity as Descartes is to the delicatessen, and no one is the wiser for it. In Germany, food keeps the umlaut alive as a characteristic of the national welfare. In Venezuela, food functions as a sanitation engineer, burning bacteria to death by the millions at any one of seven local stops on the alimentary express.

In Russia, food serves as the perfect excuse to have agriculture, for without agriculture Marxist theory would have collapsed even earlier than it did, leaving all the rhetorical paragraphs hanging around the old Politburo without a topical sentence, and forcing the Secretary of State either into nominating select parts of the original U.S.S.R. as the fifty-first United State, or reinventing Tolstoy, or both.

XII

Food as a Foremost

God's favorite human activity is said to be the spelling bee. That is because he has found that so many people cannot spell God, most particularly the French. It is a matter of some distaste to find, therefore, that the favorite (though unacknowledged) preoccupation of the French is god. Indeed, is it not said that of all the people of the earth it is the French who are preoccupied enough with god that they can take her for granted. They accomplish this by ignoring her altogether. Fortunately, close behind god is eating. It is said that once a French citizen has eaten with any authority for two or three years, always a citizen.

Even the guide books tell us that every French citizen considers himself first and hindmost a food fad. We all know that to be a fad is to be a singular event. In spite of what French movies try to show us, a French citizen tends to eat alone throughout life, and only dies in a crowd if it costs less. There is, therefore, some termination in knowing that when the French are preparing to die, they always try to eat alone beforehand, and sometimes during.

There are many reasons for this individualism, and if one were to try to give all of them, it would become unreasonable. At least one of the reasons is that the French have a formalized treaty with food, in a one-to-one relationship, and they resist interference of almost any kind. Most of all do they detest organizations, particularly military organizations, for the French like to confine their war memories to their lapels, even the women.

They reserve for those interfering military organizations the exact same relish Dreyfus mustered for anti-Semites. Nowhere is the combination of food-lover and organization-hater more obvious than in the annual French draft, when the modern draftee announces defiantly to the civil authorities, "I'm not joining while the flavor lasts."

If the national distaste for militarism in France seems awry to the average American, it is only because the French believe that any organization that attaches more importance to dying than to eating deserves to live by bread alone. They insist that a military organization adds very little to the national taste while consuming so much of it, and food is a matter of time.

The French have recently fingered, of all people, the stateside American Legion. They say it is a legion that cannot take time for food, so anxious are the legionnaires to get through peacetime, with all its dry handkerchiefs, to the salvation promised around the next corner in the defense budget. The legion would do well, they say, to remember the words of Dom Perignon, who told his men and women, "Ask not what your country can do for food, but what food can do for your country."

There are other, equally visible signs of the importance the French attach to food. Look at what it does for international haute couture. Thanks to French cuisine, it is possible to distinguish a platoon of chefs on parade from a flank of women's liberation by noticing their hats and counting the down on their thistles.

Chefs can also be differentiated from a passel of double-timing *carabinieri* because the chefs are wearing their highest decorations stained on their aprons, whereas the *carabinieri* are already sporting feathers in their caps, in deference to the ancient Italian traditions of taking credit long before it is due, and of doing anything, anytime, so long as someone is watching.

Perhaps the most fundamental contribution French food has made to the haute couture is the French uniform. The French have gained in the annals of European armed conflict a nosegay for having the most edible uniforms. This not only improves the cut of their clothes; it also explains why so many French casualties have over the years disappeared forever from the field of combat. It is a tribute to French food that the average French soldier shows greater taste in choosing his uniform than his enemies.

Unbeknownst to Americans, however, there is one transatlantic link between the American Legion and French cuisine. Each of them has introduced within its own culture the importance and resurrection of a hat. If the results are somewhat uneven, it still shows that there are many more ties that bind than can be counted four in a hand.

The Legion hat was chosen several decades ago by a National Commander whose private interest was millinery. His creation was, and continues to be, a hatter's despair, since it is pointedly inimical to the forehead, forcing the eyes into the vice of a grip so tight that when an entire American Legion post is having its annual hat day, there seem to be endless rows of eyeballs gazing at each other in sudden surprise, and they stay that way until the Lieutenant Commander, or whoever is in charge of hats, finally tells the Legionnaires that they may remove theirs.

French cuisine has had a happier effect on haute couture with its crowning accomplishment, the chef's hat, or 'la toque blanche'. The chef's hat is a perfect success because it is the perfect symbol: it looks like it just came out of the oven. The standard image of the perspiring French chef can therefore be seen in a new heat: if his forehead is aft with perspiration, it simply means his hat is still cooling.

The sad fact is that, due to cheaper ovens in Japan, most chefs' hats are now imported into France, but this should not relax our appreciation, for the greatest of the French chefs still bake their own hats daily. And when a great chef deigns to visit your table to receive your compliments, he pays you the greatest compliment of all. By leaving his kitchen's carefully balanced heat, he risks having his hat fall.

XIII

Food into Art

As we suggested in the heretofore of the Verona red tomatoes, French cuisine may not be color fast, but it is color conscious. Millions of French lifetimes are spent perfecting the hue of a turnip, the green of a lima, the roast of roast brown. Color is so important that France is the only country in the world where you have to pass the test for colorblindness before you can buy a cookbook.

Thermometers are marked for cooking temperature and color gradations. Aprons are never referred to as aprons, but as smocks, and most sauces must be made by holding in the right hand a small pastry brush, and in the left hand a pallet on which are found three shades of butter, four of onion, three of garlic, nine of salt, five of pepper, three of flour and thirteen varicose spices. No wonder French food looks as polychromatic as it sounds.

Other nations treat food colors differently. The Italians, for example, only use color as the basic scheme for the average meal. Imbued as they are with national pride, the Italians use the colors of their flag to chart the sequence. Reading from left to right, they eat red for the sauce, white for pasta, and green for the salad.

Mandarin chefs had other ideas, and took their cues from the fortunes of war and politics. So when the Emperor Wang Drop had just had another dynasty removed, the Eggs Blah would be reduced by one and would assume the traditional mourning garb of the few Chinese mourners who were ever garbed.

Even today Mandarin chefs react colorfully: when the Secretary of State sent the Deputy Prime Minister a get-well card, the brown rice turned an affable blue, but when the breathtakingly beautiful Li Gong was discovered doing her hand laundry in her bidet, the pressed ducks in Shanghai suddenly showed up corpse grey.

French interest in colorful food stems from the work of Jean-Emile Fragonard, a *pastelliste* and sometime perfume king, whose major painting, a color contrast study in violet and grunge that featured dinner for eight at Chez Scaramouche, was chosen by a national committee whose members spent two years beseeching the countryside for a canvas that would forever inspire French cooks to a reasonable facsimile, and at the same time put a mote into the eye of their Belgian competitors.

The painting was appropriately dressed for travel and hurried first to the kitchens of Louis XV, where it was depended on two meat hooks, so that whenever his majesty was temporarily disconnected from his digestive tract, he could, instead of eating, stare silently at the painting. Thus was born the genre of painting called Still Life, so named because Louis was able, by dint of his peripheral powers of concentration, to draw from a painting of inert food as much nutrition with his eyes as most people can with their noses. He grew to legend as the only European monarch to grow fat from paintings.

The Fragonard had several other beneficial effects. Entire villages learned to pool their talents, paint a canvas of food a kilometer long, and sit feeding on its beauty a half-hour daily for a year, thereby devising a practical and ultimately aesthetic response to .the starvation problem in France. Chefs were also deeply affected. They began to go to art school to learn how to design a meal, and even today great chefs spend their early morning hours sketching their next creation in charcoal on white.

Following Fra Diavolo and Leonardo's habit of enthroning themselves above a sully of novices, creating the grand scheme, and then letting the novices paint in all the numbered spaces, the important chefs of France chose assistants according to their ability to draw and design, and then taught them how to cook individual parts of the meal. When all the creations were assembled just prior to their departure from the kitchen, the master chef would with a stroke of his tongue sign the meal.

Artists rapidly took note of the beauty that was emigrating from great kitchens, and were inspired. Among them was Marcel Duchamp, one of those artists destined for every gallery and no museum, whose products must not be seen to be believed, but when believed, unseen.

Duchamp popularized the belief that the relationship between artist and artistry, prescinding from the beauty in the artist's mind, could only be apprehended by the beholder, and Duchamp had an ugly mind, however oft beheld. But he did have a role to play in the development of food as art: he introduced to each other the Fauves, a group of painters who can be said to have entered the history of French art by the kitchen door.

The Fauves were the first artists in the history of French recipes to paint the ingredients, and most of them fresh. But the Fauves got so preoccupied with the foreplay of canapes, appetizers, entrees and salads that they never made it to the desserts, and so they can only be discussed as pre-dessert artists. Nevertheless, their intimidations of fowl, hounds, leapfrogs, vegetables and weeds were a visual mouthful for the hungry French, and, since they were too expensive to be eaten, would end up as illustrations in that greatest of French art catalogues, the Larousse Gastronomique.

It came to pass that ambitious chefs spent several years in training at the École des Beaux Arts, and, while there, began to affect the *toque blanche* in order to call attention, for commercial gain, to the irregular ovality of their faces. Increasingly unhappy with merely graphic representations of food, and inspired by the fact that their costume added to their stature in the art world, these chefs began the revolutionary French doctrine of cooking an entire dinner and framing it. The dinners were then hung in a fashionable gallery, and contests were held.[5]

Judges awarded the top art prize to the painting they enjoyed eating the most: a chef's greatest satisfaction was to have his living room walls covered with empty frames. And so it was that France turned to the edible arts, developing a unique ability to digest artistic intent, yet reserving to each citizen the right to discharge artistic responsibility as he saw fit, so long as it was no shorter than three courses.

But the Bohemians tired of what they called "plain baroque" and tried to inflame it by filling their churches with aphroditic cherubim who did not seem to know which end was up. Similarly, French chefs tired of such splendid simplicities as an oyster stew and began to escalate their artistry into such

_____

5 Note that in France one can lose a contest but never quite win it.

fantasies as *Oysters à la Crème de Lionel, Fruits Fumées,* in which Lionel himself made a brief appearance, followed by billows of smoke for enfranchising the fruit. This sort of excess explains why, throughout the nineteenth century, French cuisine became so elaborate it was unrealistic, and tastebuds grew torpid and discouraged.

At its lowest ebb, when the hungry preferred to eat the frame, French food art was saved by the bareheaded appearance of that protégé of the illustrious chef Carême, Pablo Picasso, a *paelliste* who took France by force and molded its food into squares, circles, and sexagons, that is, into its most elementary shapes and tastes. Picasso's cooking was much appreciated by the dilapidated tongues of France, which styled his approach "cubism" in honor of the fact that when he was asked to cast his bread upon the soups, he fashioned the first crouton.

Unlike tradition in other countries, French tradition has the advantage of age, and many citizens who had spent their whole lives eating Fragonards found it demeaning to have to say, "Waiter, I believe there is a Cube in my soup." They could not understand why Pablo could not have invented something less modern, perhaps with some refined carving or a Louis X staircase.

Since Picasso always believed that a brushstroke in time saves nine, he finally sold his cubism to a group of cooks, and demonstrated the successful revival of France's culinary industry by putting a whole side of beef front and center in a painting of a Spanish butcher shop. It was called Guernica.

When European cooks were sufficiently exhilarated by the painting, it was sold to the Museum of Modern Art in New York in the hopes that it would inspire Americans to reinvent their national cuisine, but its only effect seems to have been that an annual pilgrimage to the painting is now required of every new employee of Armour and Company, and from time to time the U.S. Department of Agriculture stops by to stamp it "USDA Inspected Grade A Beef".

XIV

Food and Noise

Sancerre Giscard d'Estaing, the French monopolist who won forty-seven straight games by renting out all the hotels he owned on Boardwalk and Park Place *at the family rate,* once revived that he found French art reassuringly quiet. In fact, he said, it is almost as quiet as Japanese art, though not so small. It is to this element of noise as a coefficient of the relationship between food and art that we can now turn, for just as a glass of L'Hermitage is for the nose before the tongue, and a slice of Gateau St. Honoré is for the eye before the tongue, nothing is better for the ear than French food.

It is for this reason that the accomplished French cook is the one who has been taught to listen. As the saying goes, "Listen before you leap," and for the French this is a good saying as good sayings go, and better as it went. Unfavorable comparisons between the size and accreditation of the French ear and ears of other nations are so far inconclusive, but everyone will agree on this: nowhere is the value of the noise factor more audible than in a salad, and the French salad has, in this century, won more top prizes from both *Vibe* and *High Fidelity* than any other salad in captivity.

Its nearest competitor is the American salad, a totally different aural experience. Anyone in the United States who expects to serve a really memorable salad at the Saturday evening dinner party goes out and cuts the grass and the flower garden about five days beforehand and lets it lie fallow, drying to a golden, crusty brown. Late Saturday afternoon it is all raked into a large wooden bowl that has been preliminarily rubbed down with BenGay.

The salad dressings are added at five o'clock and the browns are rapidly tossed until thoroughly drenched, and the bowl is put into the freezer for about three hours. When served, this typical American salad should be eaten in unison: its noise will drown out the dessert altogether. If it is a dinner for eight, for example, the noise will be equal to the decibel count produced when a thousand square miles of thirsty Iowa corn, growing at three times its normal rate, is being trampled by a committee of the contestants from The Biggest Loser.

The French salad wins all the prizes for the simple reason that the French prefer the quality of noise to its quantity. Anyone who keeps up with *Bon Appétit* magazine can verify that the snap, crackle and pop of a fresh petunia stalk is infinitely more gratifying to the ears than the sis-boom-bah of a parched backyard. It has been said, in fact, that the French salad is more musical than the American salad in the same way Claude Debussy continues to outrank John Philip Sousa, though each has his proper pitch. The finely tuned ear is the secret weapon of the French, and whether it is listening to a salad or a bowl of noodles or the hummingbird soup, it is the only ear on the continent that refuses to listen to what it cannot eat.

The way the French keep their salad fresh right up to the moment of serving is one more lesson in solid-state audiophonics. They grow their salad in their centerpiece. This makes it a salad for sore ears, for when harvest time comes, the host uses a well-honed scythe to cut a swath through the centerpiece, letting the plants fall where they may.

Then, following the British naval tradition of picking up a seashell, putting it to the ear, and murmuring, "Yes, Your Majesty," each guest at the table picks up some salad and listens to it, and the room is soon filled with appreciative sighs: "Ah, this is a bullhorn." Or "Shh—a schizoid by Chopin!" Or "I believe this is a barge on the Meuse."

Even the average French citizen's modesty will allow the admission, "I have an ear for good food," and so the result is the French eat marvelously and noisily - they often hum in the bargain - while the tourist pedaling around France is getting used to such expressions as "He cannot see beyond his ear" or "You cannot hear as far as your mouth."

The most spectacular example of the noise factor in French food comes at Christmas, when the prices of all foodstuffs seem to rise with the star of Bethlehem. It is a curious but unassailable fact of French Christmas lore that, whereas to the wondering American eye there appear a miniature sleigh and eight tiny reindeer, to the wondering eye in France there appear a miniature sleigh and three tiny reindeer.

This does not mean that French reindeer are better fed than American reindeer and so can pull more than twice their weight. Nor does it mean that French Saint Nicks, or any other Saint Nicks allowed to visit French rooftops under the International Immunity Act, are greater lightweights than American Saint Nicks. No, these are the irregardless, the henny-penny.

The matter of fact, long known to Christmas Eve rooftop gatherers, binoculared revelers, and stowaways on the miniature sleigh, is that French reindeer have an innards strength deriving from the fact that, being less than a full team, each reindeer can make much more noise, and thereby increase the gamey quotient in his taste test.

And as every Frenchwoman enamored of all things gamier knows very well, gamier is more muscular. Indeed, urinalyses exhibited as far back as 1848 in Boulogne suggest that the average French reindeer is thrice gamier than, for example, the Laplander version, and yet is quieter and more respectful of privacy laws.

We conclude that the usual Saint Nick sleigh squad in France can therefore be reduced by Dancer, Prancer, Cupid, Donder and Blitzen. This frees the five of them for more frequent guest appearances in urinalyses boulogneses, and makes Christmas Eve in France not only twenty-five percent more calming than, say, Christmas in the Ivory Coast, but a greater taste treat.

XV

Food, Feelings, and Physiques

France is the only country in the world where the kewpies atop the wedding cake are *not* of the bride and groom, but of the chef and his wife. (The reason that both kewpies are in their formal tides is that she is also making her First Holy Communion.) The symbolism of the chef-wife couplet atop the marital icing is never lost on a French couple starting out together down the long honeysuckle vine of love.

They know that while they will average one and one-half coituses per week, and often together, they will definitely average fifteen meals together per week. So the kewpies are placed atop the cake to remind them, even during the wedding celebrations, that de Macedo's most famous marital ballade begins, "How do I love thee? Let me count the meals."

The wedding cake kewpies also illustrate quite forcefully that one of the reasons the French have been so successful with food is that they recognize where their priorities are: first, no food is neutral, and second, different foods have different feelings. For example, the ordinary garden, or sweet, pea has a very clear idea of what it is good at doing, the company it likes to keep, and how it likes to be treated.

The French have taken pains to find these things out about food and even to cater to them. The result is that there exists between food and the French a two-way communication of such mutual respect that it has taken on the dimensions of a lasting peer relationship.

And just as no relationship is without its sexuality, the French are deeply deferential, if not genuflective, towards the sex of every food-stuff, so much so that they habitually name a food by the opposite gender. The beet is female, yet they do not call it *'la betterave'* but *'le betterave'*. This is not, as the English might surprise, a cordial sidestep into transgendering.

France recognizes that male and female are but an equation of certain unpredictability, and the French are as instinctually tuned to the happy union of alternatives as a Congressman's fingers are tuned to the discrepancies twixt the pubescent and the merely adolescent, or, as the mediaevalist had it, twixt clove and hoof.

The reason for this purposeful sexual confusion is that the French recognize in all things edible and inedible an inalienable truth, – when you put a Hertz in front of an Avis, Avis tries harder. So, they put a *'la'* in front of anything masculine, to wit, – *la pomme de terre*. Every occidental realizes that there is no such thing as a feminine potato. If it were really feminine, no one would ever dream of frying it, or, worse yet, mashing it, and instead we would have ended up with potatoes gussied or, god help us, even cologned.

But the effect on the potato of carrying a *'la'* around all its life is that it tries harder to be what it already is. The French know that a potato forever in competition with itself will be healthier and tastier than the basically non-competitive potato, which only worries about occasional attacks of effeminacy.

The French believe that the strength of sexuality in food is best tapped by male chefs, for they know only too well that men are the ones who have something to lose, whereas women have the place to lose it. A woman will circle a beet for ten minutes, talking first to herself, then to the beet. She will caress and squeeze it, weighing its price, smelling it, giving it the color test, but then she will eventually turn away from it altogether.

A man will not spend time analyzing or courting any food. Instead, he will take the beet home with him for a few days and keep it around the house, where he can get used to its weaknesses and peculiarities before he decides what to do with it, since he has to know, among other things, whether the kept beet will exude or depress, for discovering the sexual identity and feelings of food is not, as Americans believe, a matter of removing the wrapper, but of knowing foods so well that, at the peak of their sexual powers, they can be introduced to each other in a fulfilling environment. The French have therefore gained for themselves a singular reputation in anthropological circles as the only people on earth who are more sexually attracted to food than to circles.

French citizens who commingle with food before eating it may be more advanced than the rest of mankind, or simply less timid. But the result is the same. They do not fear food, even when it totally disarms them. On the contrary, they want to like food, to be liked by food, and to be like food.

This democratic instinct is strongly opposed by a few of those aged White Russians in Paris whose tartar origins show only on their teeth, but it heartens everybody else, and most especially

French chefs. And nowhere in the world is the love and trust between a human being and food more firmly mirrored than in the face of a French chef.

The traveler who has seen a map of Willie Nelson's face knows that a hound and his master grow to share a strong family resemblance, to the point where it is possible to distinguish the two only by the closeness of the shave. In France, this family resemblance is reserved for a chef and his specialty. This is altogether fitting and proper, and suggests nothing scandalous or showy. The French firmly believe that it matters not how straight the plate or ormolu the bowl, a chef must look just like his food in order to show his soul.

This kind of resemblance may prove to be just the sort of advantage an ugly boy has prayed for all his life. If he was born and raised with a face that looks like it is still ripening on the vine and probably will not make it anyway, it befits him to develop Lemon Angel Cake with Spring Pickle Frosting as his specialty, though the unkind prefer to say that he is honor-bound to fit his specialty to his face and so to choose Wrinkled Cranberry Tart as his finale.

But the French also know that there are two sides to every specialty, so when an entrée arrives at the table looking like Meddled Calf's Brains in Horseradish Lavender, we know the chef is in reality as handsome as Ryan Gosling, and on all sides.

Not every French chef is born with the Gosling face, but Ryan has not yet gotten much yardage out of his puff pastry either, although Dame Judy Dench, overcome with pre-coital remorse, did once shake her rings at him when he missed a beat while transecting her metronome and caused her Yorkshire pudding to bark in her lap. Indeed, French chef training institutes, the famed 'lycées de la cuisine', which award the baccalauréat on the success or failure of a student's final bombe, have finally noted the absence of the Ryan Gosling face among French chefs, and have retuned their instruction to include several months on aestheticism in general and cosmetics in particular, for, as the leader of the Société des Lycées de la Cuisine, the American Guy Delou, said in an interview in that sobering Atlanta Constitution voice of his, "There's hardly a muthafukin Gosling at a stove anywhere in France."

Agreeing with this appraisal, the *lycées* now try to match exciting, attractive culinary creations to the needs of the student's faces. Their success is apparent years later: The great chefs of France now have a semi-annual meeting, which takes a half-year to arrange, and looking out over their faces is like reading a menu on which are listed all the classic dishes of the *haute cuisine*, but at half the price.

XVI

Food and the Psyche

The ordinarily psychic and the extrasensorially perceptive already know that the connection between food and France is the final fulfillment of Freud's lifelong search for the perfect encounter therapy. In the United States the popular expression is, "Show me what she is wearing, and I'll tell you whether she has her clothes on," but in France one citizen says of another, "Show me what he eats and I'll tell you what he digests."

This is what French psychiatrists have labeled an 'internal' view of the world, as opposed to an internal view of the universe, which is so much more internal than the world, or so it seems to those looking in from outside, even though we know not from where outside. At least this is what Teilhard de Chardin tried in his mercurial fashion to show us, once he had uncovered god stretched out alongside Andromeda between phi and omicron on his celestial yardstick.

Those with an internal view of the world take what they eat very seriously, and they tend to mold their lifestyles accordingly. It was often said, for example, that the young southern black in the United States was the perfect internalist because he was forced to sit on a fence all year long in order to be able to eat his watermelon, and he smiled between slices rather than spit the seeds out when anyone else was nearby.

Such a view is in fact a malignant interpretation of internalism, and has only encouraged Parisian psychiatrists to claim as an exemplary internalist Poitrine les Grands, the ecdysiast known for the magnificence of her double fulsome. When she peels, say the psychiatrists, she is merely extending to its professional limits her lifelong interest in artichokes.

The real lesson about internalized lifestyles is less important at the individual level, but gloriously obvious when French people are *en masse*. We remember from previous encounters that the French eat the way they dress – from the outside in – with the only difference being that they sometimes dress, though they never eat, without benefit of mirrors, even if they can dress while seated. A sidebar of the French mass mentality is that French citizens who take food most seriously for all that it has to offer will, and often do, remove all their clothes while in its presence.

Many is the foreign jaw that has become unhinged at the sudden and unexpected first view of naked French diners – a view offered most panoramically of those who dine while standing. Naked dining is nothing more than the logical extension of a basic French habit of leaving oneself exposed to the emotional implications of the cuisine.

This may lead to a surprising and quite formidable array of salutes when something delicious is served, which may in turn induce you to memorize every lap you have ever dined with, but its exasperators insist that naked dining only makes the French lap totally vulnerable to all those heated exchanges that include many a slip between cup and lip.

Whatever the pro or con, naked dining is the ultimate French tribute to the seriousness with which many a citizen treats fine food. Should the foreign visitor spot a group dining with clothed laps, the chef is probably out in the kitchen, weeping in disgrace.

XVII

French Food, French Money

Anyone who believes that a fool and his gold are soon parted does not know the French. But the adverse is also true: any fool visiting France is soon parted from his gold. It is a credit to any nation to enjoy the double advantage of keeping all its own money while desperately trying to coax everyone else into handing over theirs, and so the French have a reputation for stinginess that tends to be equalled by none and undone by few.

We can, however, note here for the first time in the history of French miserliness that all of those who are known to surpass the French in stinginess are themselves French. This agrees with Colette's famous maxim that the French always like to outdo themselves.

The excessively willing clamp the French have on their money has made the French euro the thinnest on the international market, often weak in character, but at least strong in likeness, however slim in similarity. It is a *par conséquence* and a subsequently that the French euro stretches the furthest of any metallic money in use today, for French paper money, known at the World Bank as papier mâché, has writing all over it and so burns more easily.

The French keep their money thin, not for reasons of fiscal health, but to keep their cuisine in good order, believing that a thin euro is a good euro, but that a thin euro and fat food are soon parted, for, they ask, if a man spends thin to eat fat, what doth it profit a man if he gaineth a great deal of weight and suffers the loss of his own space?

The French know only too well that one great advantage of thin money is that it takes a lot more of it to burn a hole in your pocket. Whenever good citizens gather in France, you will find in their midst a banker, saying unto them "He who eats thin, thinks fat, but he who spends thin is spending French money." It might be useful to note here that if the relationship between French money and French cuisine is not sufficiently graphic, it is at least cryptic, and the French believe that a banker who not only talks cryptic but expects to be understood must be eating right.

The conclusion that French food ultimately breeds brevity of expression is as much an enema as is the conclusion that it induces brevity of thought, for he whose thoughts stick in his throat must eventually pay the piper, and a piper paid in French money may not get fat, but at least he will not be brief in either of his thoughts or any of his expressions. So, when a paid piper gives anything a second thought, the French all know that that thought is second to none, and he himself has nowhere to go but fat.

It is for this reason, or some other, that one gets a wholly different view of the population explosion as it exists in France than as it exists, for one example, in the Bronx. The French population explosion is not a multiplying of numbers, but a redivision of space. This results from the fact that the average Frenchman celebrating his fortieth birthday occupies up to, but not including, fifty percent more space than he occupied on his twentieth birthday.

If one wishes to be genteel, one refers to this event as the miracle of the multiplication of the loaves and fishes, or as a reemphasis of food over fiscal. Whatever the explanation, France is clearly a nation of multiple girths, where their money is its own contraception and is far too often the key to imperfectly fitting clothes.

No one since Julia Roberts has tried to establish a lasting connection between the French economy and their eating habits. But it is possible that the failure of Marxism to lure the majority of the French nation away from capitalism was not in any way due to his saying, "*Labor omnia vincit*," ("The Unions Will Rise to their Own Level and Then Sink") but to his failure to say, "*Priusquam bene*" ("Above all, eat well.")

Even Marx's stepchild Question stuck her oar into the sinking ship when she turned to the audience at the Pauillac Cheese Show and thundered, "You mean no one wants to work?" Most French people still think that, when it comes to work, absence makes the heart grow fonder. All those thousands of people rushing around Marseille are not after all doing God's work, or anyone else's. They are getting ready for lunch or dinner, or whatever it is they are pre-salivating.

Had Marx's stepsister, Quotation, heard this, she would have said, "Unless you're going to say it, let me quote you." She would have been just as surprised as any American to learn that a nation can survive on its tastebuds.

Imagine the futurist Alan Tofler's shock when he first saw Paris getting ready for Thursday lunch, and realized that, at least for the Parisians, lunch superseded Thursday altogether, and at the rate of 3 meals a day, a seven-day week in the future would not only be overcome by twenty-one meals, but would eventually replace the five day work-week with fifteen meals, so that if the French kept eating at the same rate, they would not only eat themselves out of work, but finally eat themselves out of time, and would have to go back to work to give themselves a little more time for eating.

There are so many things to say about the relationship between French food and French money that if W. Steig were one day to lift himself off the pages of *The New Yorker* in order to cartoon that relationship, it would probably be the first time he had gotten any exercise since lunch, when his deep knee-bends in triplicate attracted a throng of Xeroxers. But it is not a hesitation to expose this economic fact no matter what Steig draws: the French are basically food-poor.

Being food-poor is no accident for the French. It is a conscious national policy first adopted by the French Kings as a plausible explanation of why they were fatter than Henry VIII. Being food-poor has the added advantage of distinguishing the French from other peoples: from the English, who are queen-poor; from the Americans, who are insurance-poor; from the Syrians, who are dictator-poor, and from the Chinese, who are dirt-poor. But for the French, being food-poor has been raised high in the nation's esteem; it is now next to daintiness.

Nations made of sterner fiscal fabric than France will huff and puff, and yet its house does not come tumbling down. The reason is that France has a very special contract with the World Bank. In a moment of sedentary splendor lasting right to the edge of the chair, the World Bank adopted a firm policy of forgiving any nation a fiscal weakness or two so long as they could call it a 'fiscal irresponsibility.'

It is not the purpose of the Bank to make sure that a nation cures its fiscal irresponsibility, but only to make sure that a nation has one. There is this additional alto proviso—any nation interested in having its own fiscal irresponsibility must first of all volunteer for one, and then offer proof that it can maintain whatever irresponsibility it begins.

This is in keeping with standard international monetary policy,- to allow any nation the freedom to be as fiscally irresponsible as national habits and resources will allow. The World Bank refuses, of course, as a matter of principle, to choose one of its favorite fiscal irresponsibilities and then try to get some nation to adopt it.

So, in the spirit of local option, the Bank long ago gave France the choice of how it wanted to be poor, and the French chose food. They may not have much else, including money, but food they have, and in spades. After all, just as every Islamic knee bends to Mecca each day at the sacred call, every afternoon at five o'clock millions upon millions of noses automatically turn toward Paris.

There are other factors that contribute to this poverty. The French have always assumed that since they have so much food, it must be a low-cost item. If they were dealing in mass production, this would be true, but French economists have been diverted from a serious reappraisal of just how expensive their food really is. And yet, on closer analysis, it stands to reason that if the French were paying out thin money for things costing less, they would be getting them at real value, minus par, with an additional deduction for the cashiers.

But since they are paying thin money for even the most costly items in their economy, the situation is even worse, for thin money is less inflatable because it takes less space and has less air to breathe, and so they must use more of it to pay for anything that is at high cost. In short, when the greengrocer at La Salle de Bains says the mushrooms weigh three pounds, he means they are equal in weight to three pounds of French euros, which should remind the native New Yorker of the corner newsfrau who charges you a penny a thought for the Sunday edition of the Times.

Several other observations will suffice this newly fiscal view of the French. The first is that economists must not allow themselves to be confused by the fact that the average French citizen spends every year as much money on food as the average American spends on cosmetics, making both of them a sight for sore eyes, however different the reasons and impaired the vision.

It is, after all, the responsibility of economists to be able to say with extraordinary insight and appropriately statistical charts and indices why it is they can not say anything about the economy, and so citizen spending is a useful item in their bag of tricks. What is more consequential, however, is the connection between spending and national fiscal health. When the U.S. economy fails, the average citizen's face falls, but when the French economy declines, French stomachs churn.

The second observation will be useful to economists and capitalists alike. Dyspepsia, the most peptic of the common maladies, is in a unique position to wreak considerable havoc with the French stock market. Whereas on Wall Street or in Tokyo fortunes may crumble at such newsy items as the reduced depth of the shag rug in front of George Clooney's fireplace, the French stock market is immediately in a stew when there is a half-percent lag in the truffle harvest, or when the restaurant at the Hotel de Crillon is in danger of losing a star because a frog's leg that had been accidentally sprained in the kitchen was served up in a meringue splint.

But when the crisis is not related to food, there is no economy stronger than the French. When Russia announces it has ordered a million gross plastic war helmets from Valentino, a half-dozen millionaires in places like Boston and Vienna leap to their eternal reward, but the French react only by adding a second hip bone to their beef stock, or by declaring borscht persona non grata in all France for a fortnight.

Since nothing can depress the Russians faster than the fact that the French find them ridiculous, the usual result is that, after two days, the French ambassador in Moscow submits to the President of Russia some alternate designs from Prada for a cloche military helmet in velvet, and from Laserre comes a new borscht recipe in which the borscht, solidified into the Hammer and Sickle, is sailed across a sea of beetwater on a cracker raft, and makes it to the other side.

All hands are saved; the French economy is none the worse for wear, and flavor is intact. In sum, it can be said that food impregnates the French economy, which is why family planning is de rigueur throughout France.

XVIII

Glorifying Food in France

The habit of glorifying food is as traditional in France as a haircut at the Bastille, and is closely annexed to national pride. Marie Antoinette, for example, is remembered throughout the nation as the girl who carried a whole revolution forward on the merits of eating cake. It may seem in retrospect a peculiarly oral response to an anal urge, but Marie's answer to the public starvation stemmed from her long passion for mocha and orange cake.

If her detractors repel that she should have insisted on an almond cake, it only means they are as biased as she was, but, were she alive today, they would no doubt have agreed on an orange fudge cake or a prune tart with sour cream filling as the perfect compromise.

Unhappily, but inevitably, the cake got stale, and with it sank the national pride. An Americanophile, noting the decline, likened French pride to the Thanksgiving turkey – all dressed up, stuffed to the grills (sic), and no place to go. This was further inflamed by the Archbishop of Paris, who had banished Thanksgiving forever from France as an atheists' holiday, so Americans in France had nothing godless to observe, much less to eat. They took it out on the French, and the French felt their dismay.

National leaders and courtiers alike, always quick to grab the bird by the tail, decided that the best way to nourish France's starving soul was through the mouth. They immediately inaugurated a nationwide campaign to name towns, villages, and regions of France after foodstuffs.

Anyone precursing a map of France today cannot help but notice the results: villages such as Jambon de Tournay, cities like Asperges de Nancy, and regions like Gefultefish Provence. Even an aquarium has earned a national sobriquet, less for its intrinsic food value than for the marvels cooked there. But all in all the habit of naming places by their foods allows for the obiter dictum that by their tastes ye shall know them.

One need not bury the nose in a map to glean the smells of all France. If, for example, you happen to be standing in a sidewalk *pissoir*, and your neighbor leers over the barrier to announce, "*Écoutez, caroline, je suis d'Alsace,*" ("Look, sweetie, I'm an Alsatian.") he is using nothing more than the accepted shorthand for the more correct and formal reference: "*Je suis de choucroute alsacienne,*" – which translates "I am an Alsatian sauerkraut."

The voyager in France soon learns, therefore, that all the appetizers are in the south, and as he heads north, only then does he begin the entrées. This does have its informal logic: if he forgets where he is, he has but to remember the next course in his last meal, and then go there – unless he had the mixed grill, in which case he heads for the cheapest cut, e.g. the rack of lame duck or the braised ladybug testicles, all of which tend to be to the north anyway, unless he perchance ate them after the dessert, in which case he heads south.

The only real disadvantage to this progression in appetites is that most areas of France are forced to specialize. If you are the owner of an inn near Toulouse, you specialize in hors d'oeuvres and canapés. If you own an inn in the Loire, you offer appetizers. Paris is for the entrée, and Normandy for the salad, while the perfectly serious will cross to Mont St. Michel for dessert once he has time to digest everything to the south of him. In short, the stomach has become France's most proficient traffic light.

The man who has just finished a two-week course in folding the Chicago Tribune on a crowded subway car probably expects the French to fan their passion for naming everything for food. And this is exactly what they have done. Perhaps the most memorable instance happened in the First World War, when French pilots, called '*les capots*', (the Condoms) chose to name their planes after food and thereby relieve themselves of the American tradition of naming planes after women.

The Baron Trompe L'Oeil, for example, a leading but sometimes bombardeering navigator, almost exhausted his list of prize vegetables and award-winning fruit preserves by having several dozen planes shot out from around him. The Baron had convinced his fellows that it was a far better thing they did to name a plane after an edible, for any woman worth their acquaintance would be engorged at having a plane named after her, since many of their women had the spirit of a Spitfire, but none of them looked like one.

It can now be told that it was Trompe who shot down the Red Baron with an arrow into the air, and ere it fell to earth, said Red Baron in surgery, "At least I knew where." But the biggest secret that has long been kept under hangars is that Trompe's plane, a real eyecatcher, was named "Asperges 2/1FF," meaning "You can get 2 lbs. of asparagus for a Free French franc."

Responding by popular request to national food fancies, Clemenceau, the original vituperate, said that sticks and stones could break his bones, but names should always be edible. Little did he think that this point of view would so permeate French culture as to alter the very nature of its social institutions. Food took a short journey from signposts and name tags to the heart of interpersonal relationships, and now France is the only place in the world where marriage plans are based entirely on nutrition.

This forces the French to marry with extreme care, and almost always geographically, because a boy who has lived all his life in Venison wants to find and marry a girl from Endives so as to assure themselves a lifetime entrée with salad. A girl from Fennel Tremblant will refuse the hand of a girl from Shallots Bercy because the last union of their families, in a Lamb Ratatouille, was a mitigated disaster, and further grafts between them are not advisable.

Americans will sympathize with this habit, because they exercise themselves mercilessly on marriages in order to preserve the purity of a suburban lawn or to maintain their membership in the Order of Odd Fellows. Yet it is not without a hint of fascination that Americans, careful as they are in climbing each other's family tree, watch French marital decisions revolve around the frequency of grafts, the possible extension of roots, the durability and marketability of the annual product, and the consistency of color lines.

So basic is good food sense to French marriages that the very famous wino, Marie de Chateau Margaux, married the equally wined-up Maurice de Haut-Brion strictly because he had a beautiful *tête de cuvée* that she wanted very badly. But not even this was the classic French marriage: it happened, not between

Bourbons and Bonapartes, but between two of the nation's most noble houses of entrées, when, in the early century, the direct decedent of Boeuf Bourgignon married a Filet of Sole Meunière, a union that gave birth to two famous appetizers and a groomed canapé during the decade that it took the parents to eat the dowry.

XIX

In a French Restaurant

The French are born with the taste of publicity in their mouths, and so they like to eat where everyone can see them. This may explain why the restaurant is so central to French life. They spend so much time eating out that the restaurant becomes their second home, and they treat it with the same affection, respect, and good judgment as they treat their own dining rooms. As a result, the French are very serious about the strengths and weaknesses of their restaurants; it is a country where the customers rate the restaurants, whereas in countries like the United States quite the reverse is true.

The French passion for eating in public is not at all shared by the Spaniards, who, when they eat out at all, eat very late, and in embarrassment, because the French ambassador in Madrid once remarked that they should all be ashamed of their table manners. The French, on the contrary, find public eating a challenge that rewards the enterprising and fastens the yardarms.

One of the many delights of eating in a French restaurant can be summarized in the epithet of Lamoureux, who said of French cooking that astonishment is not unakin to surprise, though they be related. The element of astonishment is especially notable in a French restaurant. Notice, for example, that most waiters and even one or two of the bell captains seem to be called Flambé. These are the ones who have raised tableside astonishment from childhood to the high art of bombast, in the very French belief that a little entertainment both opens the wallet wider and distends the digestive tract, which may, incidentally, explain why history's first sword-swallower was French.

The use of the grill and the flame in French restaurants is a remarkable achievement at any price. Not only does it keep the guests warm, but it adheres to Gabriel Faure's most famous maxim: "Good food is good theater." In short, the razzle and the dazzle in French restaurants is something quite new to the average tourist on a food toot: at its best, it can be very very good, but when it is bad it is florid, reminding us of what it must have been like to be submerged in a porcelain bathtub in Leipzig crammed full of a concert grand piano on which Franz Liszt was playing all of his Hungarian rhapsodies at once, and at full pedal.

There are a few other observations about French restaurants that will help us all. One common event is that restaurant-goers will often get excised over the surtax they are paying at the end of a check, only because they think it represents a demanded tip rather than a voluntary gratuity.

It really is nothing more than a cabaret tax that has been demanded under French law ever since Sara Bernhardt admitted, before sailing for America on her couch for her ninth final world tour of Illinois and the State of Washington, that the drama produced at the tables in French restaurants should not exceed three acts, unless she were the featured main course, in which case she could come before the nuts and right after the trained eel.

Another phenomenon is the *'corps de garçons'*. To spend three hours in a French restaurant is to understand that French waiters are required to have appeared in no less than three plays by Molière and a brace of Racine before being admitted to the bar. They continue to develop their theatrical sensitivities by serving as stand-bys in French musicals, a habit that explains for the first and last time why French restaurants close so early. But the training of the staff, while it adds to its cost, has the further disadvantage of making the patrons think they are eating in the round.

But by far the most obvious disadvantage of tableside drama is that it has effectively kept women out of restaurant jobs. When a waitress had to concoct in full view of her customers three cherries jubilee and a full order of bananas flambé, all the while watching the heat shrink her replenishments a full cup size to demi-tasse, her spirits would grow so mottled that the dew on the breast of her new-fallen pose showed the lust of her midriff and objects below. So it is that all French restaurants are characterized by the absence of waitresses; in French culinary carnivals, only men are allowed to play the clown.

When you enter any good French restaurant, you will see a man standing in the middle of the dining room with a solo finger raised as if he were summarizing a taxi to a table, or goosing an airborne gaggle. This man is the maître d'hôtel. There are those who consider the maître d'hôtel the bellwether of French cuisine. His singular responsibility is to maintain successful tableside cooking by testing the wind patterns inside the restaurant, so it is often said of the successful maître d'hôtel's fingers that many are cold, but few are frozen, and a good thing, too.

This man's index finger is often the most highly insured item in the restaurant, with Lloyd's offering a two-for-one sale on a double indemnity. The double indemnity is twice important because the index finger sometimes retires from service before the rest of the maître d'hôtel. In fact, when a maître d'hôtel has lost his index finger into retirement, he is thereafter known as the maître d'.

A maître d's success as a guide to the wind patterns is essential to both tableside artistry and customer comfort. If, for example, the entire South corner of the restaurant is filled with sanitation engineers from Portofon, who are exhaling at a faster rate than they are inhaling, it follows that the opposite, or West, corner suffers, for with such a gale the fat is soon out of the fire and into their laps. Some restaurants have tried turning on fans to counteract a prevailing wind of that kind, but the fan only produces a host of unexpecteds.

One unexpected was when an antique anemometer spinning wildly atop the flagpole outside *Chez Coquette* turned out to be the brassiere of that gilded swan, the Vicomtesse de Ribes. Another happened near Table 19 North at *Le Brassy*; the fans suddenly caught a seersuckered Honoré Le Grand in a downdraft, and there eddied out across the dance floor his custom-made pubic hairpiece, with the label side up. It read: "This isn't fake anything. It's real pubic Dynel."

Wind patterns have made it important in France for the average restaurant-goer to time his arrival exactly, and to know in advance not only which table he will have, but which seat, and for how long. He will also consider the age and weight of his expected waiter, his average kitchen-to-table times over the past ten months, and the thickness of his heels.

As one might expect, the arithmetic of all this planning for dinner out often graduates to calculus, and families have been known to spend the entire week getting ready for Saturday's restaurant dinner with slide rules, compasses, and erasable napkins, plotting the graph from the door to the least windy table at their favorite restaurant.

But geometry alone cannot brunt the full responsibility. Weather reports are analyzed and astrologists are consulted nationally. Those who do not have time to struggle maturely with the statistics of dining out can of course stay home, hang a flaming brandied orange rind on their crust of Limburger cheese and call it the Eve of St. Joan.

Or they can appear at the restaurant door attired in those yellow paraffin exclamation coats and the Cape of Good Hope brimmed hats, thereby signaling that they are willing to take a chance with the fans, or to be willing to take a table to the west of all those sanitation engineers exhaling westward.

The French know how to handle their own wind problems, but if you are a tourist dining out, and the winds inside your eatery blow you some ill, there are one or two gambols that are well worth carousing. You can point very loudly to your soup, which by now is swollen into cresting waves, and trumpet to the room at large: "See those poor devils struggling to stay afloat in the midst of this gale? Those are salmonella bacteria."

This usually creates an instant downswell as the maître d'hôtel, dashing to your side, gets sucked into a potted palm by the sudden vacuum created by the disappearance of all the other diners. But this gambol has a disadvantage. He who stays behind because he fears not salmonella is morally submerged into adding another 15% to his billed gratuity, and must mumble something entertaining like "*Vive la différence*" or "*À bout de soufflé*" in jest as he parades out.

This is an extreme gambol, to be used only when the draft around your table is damaging your dithyramb so badly that you can hardly breathe. A less extreme gambol has been designed by Maurice Lefevre, the sports enigmatic whose astrodome was said to be built on pennies from heaven. Maurice solves the whole tableside grill problem at *Les Pyramides* by serving everything outdoors while keeping the guests locked indoors.

Then, at a given signal, he lets them all rush outside, once through the parking lot, out across a Japanese pebble garden, and into a waiting bus, which collects the standard fare for short rides, cautions them against smoking in front of the white line, and lets them exit via the rear door, where they find their food cool but waiting, and partially eaten, though never in vain.

Giles Guile, the owner of the famed *Argent Massif* near Limoges, had his own gambol. He tackled the problem of internal winds by teaching his staff not to huff and to puff or they would blow the place down. Then, taking a different stance, he sat at the doors between the kitchen and the main dining room, with a stopwatch and a gastronome in hand.

After three weeks of clocking and measuring the average draft created by waiter inputs and outputs, he decided that indoor grilling could be maintained if waiters would put the food trays on small fire-red wagons, and pull them out into the dining room to the waiting customers. Since wagons would slow down both inputs and outputs, Guile correctly induced that the draft ratio inside his restaurant would go down to the sea in ships, and it did.

XX

At the Table

Getting to the table in France is only half the battle, though it can be more than half if the featured wind of the month is the sirocco or the mistral. The other half of the battle is staying there. One particularly divisive element is the fact that the French eat with the fork in the left hand and the knife in the right. The result of this fickle custom is that belligerence long ago graduated from the boxing ring and the wrestling pad to the far more urbane, if not sometimes alarming, art of two-fisted dining.

It is helpful to know that Catherine de' Medici, known as *The Italian Transplant,* is believed to have enunciated the custom of the right-handed knife because she was right-breasted, while the average French citizen tends to be left-lipped, which seems to have come from a biologically habitual failure to speak on both sides of their opinions.

The primary effect of eating from the dueling position is that the French tend to cut everything on their plates at least into halves, and sometimes into wholes, and the first time a stranger watches a French diner cutting his salt, cultural shock fills the air, which, by the end of a long meal, is already thinly sliced, since a doubly-armed Frenchman exercises his conversation so skillfully with knife and fork that his punctuation quickly escalates from the paragraphic to the jugular.

The French may sharpen their conversation as a prelude to cutting their meat, but they also believe that to look sharp every time they eat, to feel sharp and be on the ball, to be sharp they must use a blade with the sharpest edges ever honed. The best French knife has a double edge to it and is called the *'entendre'*, which is a messy word having to do with sutured gizzards and should not be often exposed in bare print.

The desirability of the double edge is that it gives its handler the advantage both coming and going, and just after Yvonne has lunged a foot beyond the *Compote de Fruits* and stabbed a shabby remark about Paul Verlaine straight through the apoplexy, she can retreat on a point of honor made by a dinner guest outside the reach of her surgical field, and attend thereafter to the parsley twigs growing out of her custard relish.

The effect of all this is that the French believe, however infirmly, that cutlery makes the food grow fonder, and as penchants from the Midi always say, "The fonder the food, the tastier the meal, but the harder they fall." Diat, one of the country's most kitchen inventors, noticed that his fellow countrymen brandish their dinner weapons the way the Chinese brandish their factories, and insisted that every meal in France be served within its borders, so that it could at least start with a peaceful hors d'oeuvre and whenever possible remain outside the field of combat, or *'hors de combat'*, throughout the meal.

If, therefore, one steps into France and hears a national anthem of utensils clashing over the dinner tables, one can be comforted knowing that the food may be getting cold, but someone is winning.

A cluster of cutlery above the table is also stimulus enough to produce in French cuisine an ardent flavor that rises over the general population like the forehead of Malraux. But perhaps it is not enough of a rationale, as it fails to account for social class.

The French like to think that a certain finesse with one's knife and fork is a mark of superior family background, and distinguishes them from such of their borderlines as the Germans, who try to preserve their genealogical charts by wearing to public occasions one or two small saber scars about the mouth, so that lesser-bred Germans can tell that a silken aristocrat may purse his mouth, but the scars tell the true story of their carelessness with any kind of knife.

But when it comes to pride, the French dispense altogether with cosmetics. A family member who feels his clan has been tainted can resurrect its honor, not with anything so heavy-handed as a saber, but by a solo virtuose at the dinner table, in which he carves with his right hand an entire game of tic-tac-toe on a half-inch pat of butter, and wins, while with his left hand he scales a scallion spray so extraneously that the spray remains aloof.

Many people suppose that anyone who takes their food that seriously does not talk while eating. This is a sheer suppository, and it goes where it belongs. The French have far too much self-respect to be quiet in the presence of anyone or anything, seeing silence as a mark of a boor among mankind and a fool with food.

They have also learned that, even if one is in direct conversation with one's baked oysters, the further enjoyment of food depends on where one sits. If one sits at the seven o'clock position, for example, and begins the courtesies to one's neighbors, time passes so quickly that one's appetizer has moved on to eight o'clock, and by the time one finishes thanking three o'clock for the anchovy paste and coriander, one's entrée is already past eight o'clock and heading for nine.

The French, therefore, practice defensive eating. When ten French citizens besiege a table with their stomachs erect, they brandy their flatware about, and you can be certain they shall reap, for no matter how much they look like a frieze from a Millet harvest scene, they are not there to be picturesque. They are fully armed because they know that when their food arrives in front of them, this is their one and only chance to eat, and they have no intention of letting anyone else do it for them.

The apparition of a French dinner table as an armed camp of war is not the vision the Plaza Athénée wants to conjure up to attract the contemporary tourist trade. If anyone had the idea that dinner in France could get nasty, it was only by imagining a battle between customer and waiter, or waiter and maître d'hôtel, or between hostess and butler. But no one ever imagined it would be among guests.

Yet it is perfectly logical: if a guest predicates the success of a dinner in France on whether or not he has succeeded in fending off an attack on his food by another guest, then the result is a national habit of two-fisted dining that makes a meal anywhere in France tantamount to a *tête-à-tête* with the Grim Reaper. Walking away from the table, a guest may or may not recall the food, but he can describe in great detail the guest or guests who never got a chance to eat it.

Seating rules do not only apply to the guests, but to the hostess, who for example would never eat on Greenwich Time while her guests are eating on Central Standard Time. Nor does she ever sit at the 12 o'clock position, because if she starts her party at eight o'clock, she would have to wait four hours before she could eat, and when her entrée arrives, it will find her in a more than usual phase of utopia, such as was never induced by Saint Thomas More – a utopia known among the French as the twelve o'clock high.

The hostess is thereby advised to entertain at a round table, where the equidistance between guests will be spaced accordingly, except that the adroit hostess will seat at the half-hour any guest who has a pressing departure, with the understanding that he will receive but one-half his due, unless other guests consider his departure overdue, in which case he will be underfed.

But if the table is longer than it is wide, it will take the guest at four o'clock, for example, more time to pass the Glazed Ginseng to five o'clock than it will take five o'clock to pass it to six. Therefore, anyone who is all wound up should be seated no later than the nine o'clock position so as not to interfere with the timing of the meal.

But anyone using the meal as an occasion to wind down should either arrive early or pass all the food counterclockwise, except that purists will prefer to change their watches to the right hand and eat the first course left handed, unless there is a butler, in which case the dissatisfied guest sets his alarm wristwatch for sixty seconds and announces, just as the plate is being placed, that any forthcoming tinkle automatically signals a pollution count in high excess of the lung-collapsing zone, a maneuver guaranteed to wind down the service and wind up the party.

XXI

The Elements of Good Dining

A final note on French dining will help give the illusion of finality. It used to be said that a real gourmet was the only one at a dinner party who was seated between the entrée and the salad so as to get a fair view of the proceedings. This was disputed by a small band of tongue-tied swoons called "The Forkists", who claimed that the true gourmet was the only one at the table who did not need to use her cutlery to fend off ravaging guests, since she had already delivered the *'coup de nausée'* (a threatening gesture aimed at lightly penetrating the stomach) to over a dozen guests at previous dinners by arming herself with an aura of bad breath so finely honed as to turn the wine to vinegar even before the cork was out.

By not denying these were the traditional definitions of a French gourmet, we can skip controversy and pass on to the far more lucid definition now popular throughout France and now eddying out in the general directions of both Sydney and Cochabamba : The gourmet is the person who is able to advise a host or hostess on the appropriate weather for particular groupings of food.

The French are the first to have introduced weather into the dining room. They consider it the perfect complement to quality cuisine. They used to prefer imported weather, and particularly the English weather that sparked such widespread commentary, ranging from the spoken to the oral, when it was introduced into France in the 1600's after the English found themselves with an excess of it. But now that national pride swells anew, the chic hostess chooses for her dining room a domestic weather pattern from among the available brands in the local diningroom weather market.

It is as hard for a Frenchman to picture a meal without weather as it is for an American to tip a mortician, for weather, as Noilly-Prat would have said, is almost everywhere. But just because the hostess chose it doesn't always mean the weather is going to work. The Treaty of Versailles was almost lost when, the night before its signing, the Marquise de Sade wanted fog for her Chicken Alba, and got a hail-storm instead.

Likewise, under adverse circumstances, the preferred thunderstorm over the grilled lamb chops *vert pré* does not always materialize, leaving the bereaved hosts to cope with a paintpeeling display of electricity, but no rain, and no thunder. The French adoption of weather is of course the legacy of Benjamin Franklin, the electrician, who opted to Paris for his junior year abroad and earned himself a place in France's undiluted affections by introducing lightning, on call, into the dining rooms of France.

Indeed, flocks of passerby tourists can be seen even today gaping with eyes abug through French dining room windows at the vision of hostesses and cooks galumphing around their dining room tables, flying kites. Although rumors that this is the authoritative explanation of the origin of the cliché, "cooking up a storm," are ungrounded, it is true that several other rumors have recently been found, but it is now known they do not refer to this cliché.

They concern the statistically probable possibility that the Electrical Institute's semi-periodic survey of French dining rooms shows that more wall sconces are grounded in France than in any other nation, which could prove France is the paramour of the Enlightenment. We can only conclude that its future could be brighter still if only they would turn the food up higher.

So in order to disable the reader as gently as possible, we begin with a few Helpless Hints, intended for those who do not have any domestic help, or for those who do but think they do not, or for those whose help have no help but think they do not. Helpless Hints are not intended for those who do not have any help but think they do, nor for those whose help have no help but think they do.

The hints to be found in the following pages are hints on the order of a stage whisper. They are nothing more than hints in the right direction, and do not pretend to be any the less exhaustive for being suggestive. But these hints do intend to leave the helpless reader with the feeling that there is never much help for anyone, but whatever help there is can certainly use some more, and might have even gotten it here.

XXII

By Their Names Ye Shall Know Them

The perverse defector of French food will say of the French connection between food and language that, if you take away all the fancy names, the food will lose its taste. The subsidiary of this point of view is that, if you mispronounce the names, the food tastes quite different. That is why the famous chef Francois Couperin once said, "I carry my food as an adornment on my clothes."

The only reason a statement of this unusual an ilk could be made at all is that the French long ago had to face up squarely to the problem of whether it is nobler to make the name taste like the food or the food taste like the name, a problem not unlike that inherent in the famous dilemma, "Which came first, the chicken or the egg?" – a dilemma unresolved to everyone's stupefaction by a simple French rephrase: "Which came first, the sunnyside up or the egg?"

Following their former footsteps, the French solve the problem of naming foods with the double deft of spelling everything they eat and eating everything they spell – with this exception, that if they cannot spell it properly, they eat something else. This leads us right from start to finish, for if anyone believes that language be the food of love, then the French be the world's fattest romantics.

Naming anything edible is a matter of taste but an occasion for flair. There is nothing precise or mathematical about it; if there were, the French would perpetually carry slide rules in their mouths. The rite by which foods are baptized is so complex that to describe it would take a textbook fat enough to make the average French cookbook look like a 97 lb. weakling.

Nevertheless, there are some basic, though not fundamental rules for naming French food, which, once learned, are difficult to remember. They will be given later so as to shorten the span of time during which they might otherwise be forgotten.

But first, by popular demand, and as an appetizing entrée to the food names mystique so popular with the French nation here and abroad, we must understand that some food names happen quite accidentally. Perhaps the most nominal example of this occurred in 1813, when a pastry chef named Crêpe de Chine learned that the highest ranking of all French generals, a Corsican everyone called Little One-Hand, was approaching the pastry shop on all threes.

It happened that Chine had that morning finished a life-size, puff-pasted rectangular monument to the Duke of Wellington that stood as erect as a marine in a group shower and had a yellow custard waiting by its side. Crêpe had intended to sell his new creation to the Irish for excremental purposes, but he was no fool. The advent of a sweet-toothed general in need of some moral and physical refreshment, and perhaps even a nip and a tuck of fame, could be his Waterbrook or his Donnyloo, but, if the pastry pleased the general, it might make them both famous.

Flipping the Wellington on its side, de Chine painted it from stem to stern with vanilla frosting, and engorged the layers with the custard to make it seem even fatter than it was. Then, just as the Greatness himself crept in, Crêpe pointed proudly to his new artistry, and fired the words heard round the nation ever since, —the words that made that commanding general into a minor but permanent French deity: *"Pour vous, mon général – le premier Napoléon!"*

Crêpe's gesture was a spur-of-the-moment, and a risk of sorts, but the important thing for the future of French pastry and the immortality of Napoleon is that it worked. However, their mutual felicity cannot be allowed to obscure an eclipse. Most names of French food are the result of deliberations as long and dramatic as those between two married American suburbans choosing a new life-insurance policy, and only then, when promises and hopes waver between compromises and concessions, do all the beguiles of the French character come home to roost. But this is only true when a totally new creation is being baptized.

If the object in question is merely a mutation, or a variation on an existing delicacy, it does not get an original name. One of the two basic French solutions is to add to its existing name the date of its birth. For example, if Calf's Addle has the original addle intact, but varies from the original in being baked as far as mid-way, then it becomes Half-Baked Calf's Addle 1972.

The second solution is to play some impromptu variations on the existing name and hope they come out all right. The very last such attempt was a spellbinder in which the original

Vol-au-Vent became Vol-au-Vol-au-Vent, as in the more canta-bile, "Vol-au-Vol-au-Vent a penny a pitch."

Diving into the mystery of food names before knowing some-thing more about French food preparation is tantamount to a reversal, when just a few alterations alter one's thought to fit one's taste. The first thing anyone who is going to take a dive should do is to make sure to have at least a swimsuit on. This is as necessary for French food as it is for a British marriage, for whatever it is, new or old, almost everything served on a French table is either swimming in something, or drowning in it.

The French penchant for naming every little thing they eat can therefore be seen as one way to solve the otherwise terri-fying problem of identifying whatever it is that is either swim-ming or drowning, and thus to know whether it is supposed to be drowning or should in charity be saved, for the French perpetuate the notion that it is two days of bad luck to watch a food drowning, but only half a day of bad luck if it arrives at the table already drowned, whereas three thousand Frequent Flier miles go to anyone who rescues a food from its sauce. This is in accordance with the French belief that a rescued food always tastes incomparably vivacious for the first few minutes after it has been rescued, and so should be eaten instantly.

The usual way French culinary architects create a new dish is by taking one of the classic tried and true golden oldies of the haute cuisine and adding mushrooms: This is called the "face-lifting" school of food architecture. If mushrooms do not do the trick all by themselves, the architect merely says that she has added a garland of mushrooms, so that a salmagundi & mush-rooms may be a better salmagundi, but a salmagundi & *garland* of mushrooms is thereafter referred to as *Élégance de Salmagundi Uma Thurman.*

The other school of French food architecture is the "face-saving" school, which combines the safety of the familiar with the intrigue of the secret, so that anyone approaching what looks from afar like a duck will, when as close as the eyes may see, mutter, "For crying out loud, this is just plain old Roast Forelocks of Caneton à la Martiniquaise."

What he soon discovers is that hidden underneath are the secret ingredients, the very stuff of which originalities are made – in this case, four unshelled peanuts and a half-dozen stiffened squid joints in myrrh. An equally inspired example is Tuna on the Half-Shell, in which a home-grown tuna fish salad is stuffed into a pack of snail shells straight from the aquarium or the backyard. Preferred here are the empty snail shells so popular with exiled starfish; they can be checked for emptiness by carrying them into a dark room and trying to see the whites of their eyes.

When the empties are made whole again with tuna salad, the snail exits are then blocked with wads of cotton soaked in gin, the shells are sprinkled conservatively with one of the darker paprikas, and the snail pack is then served anytime after the meal with great fanfare. If fanfare is not readily available, try borrowing some from a neighbor. But if all else fails, so will this.

Anyone who takes even a brief course at either of the two schools of French food architecture is ready to name names. It was, after all, a French poet, Mal Armé, who said that it matters not how strait the plate nor smeared with marmalade the roll, a French meal is adjudged first-rate if the food names all have soul. And if it is true that, by the time you figure out the names of all the dishes in the French classic cuisine you will hardly have any taste for the semi-classics, then it is double in import to understand that there is as much etiquette to naming a dish as there is to eating it, though less than to cooking it.

The first rule in understanding and creating French food names is this: Honor the preposition. This is particularly easy for Americans, because they have been taught throughout childhood to look for the helping verb, and so they have a razor's edge eye for all those little words that carry a big stick. The French preposition *'au'*, for example, is used to signal the presence of a dominant spice or flavor. *Steak au poivre* means essentially a peppery steak, one that weakens just before the sneeze.

The preposition *'aux'* signals the presence of several dominant spices, as in *pommes de terre aux harlequins*, a border dish of potatoes starring a multicolor of tutti-frutti beneath the skins. Sometimes the *'aux'* is deceptive; it can mean that the featured article is cloaked in something, like anchovy skins or fried lilies.

On the other hand, the preposition *'en'* is our ambivert. *'En'* *#1* means the food is cloaked in something, all right, but it is probably not fried lilies, like *potaqe en masse*, or a mess of pottage. *'En'* *#2* usually means that there is something hidden in the middle, like *gigot d'agneau en papillote*, which is a wolf sewed into sheep's clothing.

The preposition *'à'*, the smallest of the culinary prepositions but by far the most heavily accented, is a casual handy, and just in time. When joined with the single *'la'*, as opposed to the double *'la'*, or what it is now known as the *'la la'*, this tiny preposition forms the *'à la'*, which is less a dental than a labial. The *'la la'*, on the contrary, almost never follows the *'à'*, since the *'la la'* is at its best when sung, except when it follows the *'aux'*, as in *'aux la la'*, an exclamation used by singing French citizens whenever they burn their tongues.

When the *'à la'* stands alone, it is at least half a sound for sore tongues, and it hints at foreign flavors, so that *Tripes à la Bouillabaisse* means tripe with that smoky, round-shouldered flavor so common to the arrowroot forests of Bouillabaisse. When the *'à la'* joins the *'mode'*, it is used *'à la mode'* to suggest the presence or the remembrance of ice cream, and when it is *'à la mode de'* something, as in *'à la mode de Caen'*, it is a zingy, because this means that Caen ice cream is being used.

The expression *'à la mode'* is not to be confused, however, with the more vehicular *'à la carte'*, which simply means that any culinary gem heavy enough to be wheeled in to the room will be more savory if it is cooked in your lap.

Anyone who thinks there is nothing more to dishing up French food names than gluing them together with dazzling prepositions can easily be mistaken for a fool. The second major rule in naming French food is this: Beware the capital letter. A capital letter means either that this particular food has been imported from another country, or that it has been improved upon under the tutelage of the chef's wife, whose name is inscribed thereon in full caps.

A capital letter also reveals that the creator, or, as the sex may be, the creatrix, is still uncomfortable with sex. Small letters, on the contrary, mean that the dish was created somewhere far out in the provinces and has finally made it to Paris, which, with its traditional glitter of art nouveau, always decorates itself with things provincial but spells them in small letters to help keep them in their place.

There are, of course, too many variations of food names to vary here. One need only consider the difficulty in distinguishing an ordinary duck, a *canard,* from a *caneton,* which is nothing more than a *canard* with its tonsils removed, to know that one cannot cover the whole index of names. But since two are definitely better than one in this regard, there are one or two other hints that will help you to relax into a French menu. The first is that a *filet* is anything from which the small bones have been removed. The second is that a *filet mignon* is anything from which the prettiest of the small bones have been removed.

These removals will clear the throat for the sauces, which, as the French know, are very hard to get to know. French sauces are so similar in appearance that a Mandarin chef once complained that all French sauces looked alike to her. This explains the lengths to which the aggrieved French have subsequently gone in giving each sauce a distinctive name.

The secret to all the French sauces is in their names, and not in their tastes. If the name has an accent on the semi-final vowel, as in *'sauce adorée'*, it is probably brown, or at least it once was. If the accent is up front, it is probably a white sauce, or at least a few will fervently hope so. If the name is short, as in *'sauce aha'*, it means the sauce is thick. But if the name is long, as in *"sauce aux grands petit-pois à la manière de Victor Huguenot, Jr."* it means the sauce is slender, and full of air, perhaps with even a shrug of pretense. In any case, the quickest and easiest route to a full command of every French sauce is to say the name of the sauce aloud. And if you say it right the first time, don't eat it.

Having said all that, it only remains to note that the French believe there is no incompatibility between their traditional democracy and a class consciousness that is as free of high-and-mightiness as the previously-regnant d'Orléans gang. They have accordingly established this rigid hierarchy in naming foods:

Battles before Places
Places before Courtesans
Courtesans before Mignons
Mignons before Age
Age before Beauty
Beauty before Beasts
Beasts before Cousins
Cousins before Nieces
Nieces before Priests
Priests before Bishops
Bishops before Cathedrals
Cathedrals before Metro stations

Metro stations before Cats
Cats before Dogs
Dogs before Sex
Sex before Death
Death before Sinners
Sinners before Saints
Saints before Pearls
Pearls before Swine
I before E (except in a C food)

This astonishing array of the proper positions of words incorporated into French food names illustrates all too vividly the failure of the Americans to give enduringly appropriate names to new wonders from their kitchens, and is proof positive that one must have the knack for names, for if imitation is the root of all evil, then nothing succeeds like failure. A brief glance, by category, at some of the new names in American food will demonstrate how far amok the puck can sail:

Category	Final Choice for Dish Name
Ethnic	Blackeyed Peas Kanye West
Artistic	Potato Dumplings Kate Moss
Politic	Filet of Sole Herman Cain
Athletic	Hot Dog in Brine Barry Bonds
Medical	Foreskin of Bandaged Pork George Bush
Socioeconomic	Freshly Coined Mint Ben Bernanke
Physical	Double Butt of Seated Beef Rush Limbaugh
Pietistic	Lamb of God Billy Graham
Forensic	Autopsied Brains Sarah Palin

Clearly, food names are not an American métier. These deserve the anonymity for which they have become so famous.

❧

XXIII

Tis the Season

Anew expression rapidly gaining circulation among the
food lovers of the world summarizes another of the
many food lessons France gives to all other nations
under God. It is this: Spice is the variety of life. The botanically
inept will assume that this means France grows everywhere
brown and verdant with the spices of the occident and the
orient. In fact, France is virtually bereft of home-grown spices.

Whether this is because of the traditional mildness of French
attention or the harshness of the national breath we do not
know. But this we do know: French cooks buy huge amounts of
imported spices, and have given more variety to the life of spice
than the folks at Enron have given heartburn to the Internal
Revenue Service. And this is no mere accomplishment. It is a
fait accompli.

The overuse of spices in the preparation and consumption of food is considered by those whose tongues have been

educated beyond Sesame Street to be as fundamental as ignorance among the Teabaggists. Consider for a moment the alternative – American food. The absence of spices in American food is commonly referred to as the Cracker Barrel perplex, and it is often the object of a great deal of jolly.

The perplex represents this phenomenon: any American traveler on any American road is able to taste anything served in a restaurant at least forty miles before he gets there. The French would call this phenomenon foods anonymous at its best. You don't even have to eat it to be bored by it.

Indeed, the French consider any kind of predictability a pox on the tongue, and for good reason. The normal French tongue is coached at its most naked age to discriminate among seasonings as soon as they are introduced into the mother's milk, so that if the baby is balking at the breast, the French pediatrician advises the mother to switch to oregano or dill weed or turmeric for a few days. As it grows, the average French tongue acquires a maturity far beyond its years, and by the age of twenty an otherwise dull French citizen can tell forty spices apart by sight, fifty by smell, and sixty by taste.

At the age of thirty, a tongue showing unusual abilities, and not busy elsewhere, is given the vainglorious 'Spicemeister' test, a remnant of the Franco-German amity sale after the World War and first performed by Jurgen Catnip in his imbecile near Spidersee. In this particular rambunctious a different spice is put on each key of a concert grand keyboard, and the contestant's tongue is given three minutes to lick the whole thing clean, naming each spice as it goes, and at the end announcing the piece just played.

But even the French know that a complete command over the whole rack of available spices is only the very next thing to possible, while helplessness among the spices is the rule in most other nations, with the flaming exception of Thailand, where a special squad of firefighters is devoted exclusively to the mouth.

In other words, helplessness among the spices cannot always be cured, but it can be conquered. The first and the foremost is that all spices are divided into the greater and the lesser spices. The French believe that the greater spices come from the West and the lesser spices from the East.

They describe Western spices as rangy and ebullient, with greater respect for food, while describing Eastern spices as lesser because they are smaller and more delicate, with a tendency to look alive. The sporty and yet awkward Western spices are given to the grand gesture no matter how slim their chances, whereas Eastern spices grow less pungent the farther they are from home.

Nevethemore, Eastern spices sometimes taste like a cozy of lye being put to the torch just north of the tonsils, whereas a Western spice like rosemary is normally so pacific that, when it is in retardation, it takes a whole clarinetful of the stuff to make a thin turkey leg talk back to its owner.

It is accordingly a deft and a manual to be able to mix the Eastern and Western spices in such a way that neither is the lesser and the former is the latter. The problem of achieving a balanced mix has to the present day been the province of the master of nuance and the mistress of chance, - titles the French also give to the stars of their National Assembly.

But it is too soon to say that the mix is none too soon, though it is not too late either, for in the matter of mixing Eastern and Western spices French tradition dictates that the sooner the better, and perversely, never is later – and this is even truer of spices than anyone suspects.

Any lovable French cook will tell you that spices are in the eyes of the beholder, and that spices in the hands of a benevolent cook will not necessarily do any harm, though spices in the hands of a bellicose cook are not going to do anyone any good, either. This makes it easier to understand why spices can be better in the hands of the beholder. A better spice is devoutly to be wished, for if any food creation is to grow up right, the question of correcting the seasonings will inevitably arise early in its life.

The assumption that seasonings need correcting is a reprehensive going back to the time when the infamously unraveled scarf addict, Robespierre, whose concierge Madame Lafarge taught him to "Cut a stitch in time, till leap year bring you twenty-nine," introduced his nation to the cleanest shave this side of Gillette, and reinstituted to its former popularity the butcher's block.

Robespierre, an astound by temperament but a profound by chance, came to be known by his name because he had a habit of being called. True to his ancestry and a weak will, he knew that, though many were called, being called was at least the first step to being chosen, though he might have preferred that only a very few be called, and fewer still be chosen, which would have given his chances of being both called and chosen a mathematically significant leap in some direction, thereby consternating his critics, who already felt he laced his boots too close to the water on his knees.

One would imagine that the idea of correcting seasonings as a basic tenet of ethics would have appeared to at least one of the French Illuminati long before Robespierre. The Illuminati had already profited, after intense observation, from the discovery that Henry VIII's conscience was in the shape of a sexagon, so they could hardly be called strangers to the dilemmas of a strawberry blond.

But history shows that, of all the Illuminati, only Rousseau and Rochambeau dealt head-on with the problem, though mercifully not with each other. Their interest should come as no surprise, since they are known to have been gluttons for ethics. Nevertheless, French cookbooks still record the amaze that the moral dilemma of food was so acute for both of them that, in their final six decades, neither gentleman was able to decide the proper direction in which to correct a seasoning. They ended their days staring at each other and hungry, unless either was seated.

The ability to correct seasonings is generally considered by American psychologists to be an acquired taste rooted in one's genetic code and brought to full florence by select childhood traumas, or by the disciplined behavior one learns while being raised by proxy in a private school. Although numerous experiments conducted in the Lean Cuisine Kitchens tend to confirm that diagnosis, the French know better. Recognizing that the choice of correcting or not correcting your seasonings is fundamentally a moral issue, they accept the fact that everyone must first learn to distinguish between right and wrong.

If this explains why French citizens themselves are often distinguished between right and wrong, it explains even better how it has come to pass that the curriculum of the entire French public school system has balanced heroically for centuries on the fulcrum of one prepossessing moral predicament: i.e. to correct or not to correct the seasonings.

It is not exactly in effluvium, therefore, to say that the backbone of French character, and one or two of its sphincters, have been built on that singular choice. And since the stronger the seasonings, the greater the need for correction, French food has tended to emphasize the muscular seasonings over the musical, in the belief that a well-braced stew not only aggravates the hairline and sinews the thigh, but gives French youths an opportunity to resort to moral choice whenever they are called upon to make the family supper.

In light of the pedagogical values of cooking, it is rightly said that, if the spice trade were to die tomorrow, French education would be in ruins by the end of the week. And so the pollywogs, who are already decrying the influence of the Michelin star on French suicide statistics, will want to develop this correlation to its ad nauseam by estimating whether there is any significant relationship between a teaspoon of chervil, a tablespoon of chervil, and France's cultural survival.

In China, the correcting of seasonings is left to the calendarians, and in Indonesia to the typhoonists, but in France it is generally entrusted to cooks. Singled out for particular responsibility are the more experienced cooks, who are usually called chefs, though the more unusual are addressed as Monsieur or Madame, because they roll up their sleeves when washing their hands of it, which accounts for the total absence of cuff buttons, and the total presence of forearm hair, in many of the more drinkable French *'digestifs'*.

These famous Monsieurs and Madames are revered throughout France for their realism with spices. First of all, they know that if you have any intention of correcting your seasonings, you must control your temperature. They also know that many spices are like the theology of the Watch Tower Society, in that they suggest so much more than they can deliver. But most of all they have the Eighth Sense, or what is known among the Anglos and the Saxons as the Moral Mandible, which means they just *know* when the seasonings require correction.

Of course, any spice worth its salt is not going to sit around waiting to be corrected. There is no masochism in spices, and the French know it. They also know that spices are prone to sneaking off before anyone has had a chance to correct them. Indeed, some food culturists have said that everyday French cuisine is too often marked by the ghosts of departed spices. As usual, however, the French chef has a practical solution to this problem when it arises. He sets the dish in the middle of an aluminum foil square and circles it slowly for half an hour, squashing the escapees.

But the ruination of spices in flight is not to be mistakenly considered as the *ne plus ultra* of the accomplished French chef. It is in fact considered by its critics to be the trademark of those who cook by retribution, or what might in the United States be called the McDonald's syndrome, in which food art has never graduated from the disciplinary to the inspirational, but has instead become a wholehearted revenge upon those who eat it, and an everyday reminder that in some nations, especially the United States, the act of swallowing is assumed to be the equivalent of tasting.

In France, on the contrary, revenge cooking is not the custom, and it is not characteristic of most chefs to return home after a long day over a hot stove and tell their wives they had the pleasure of squashing altogether three ounces of ersatz seasonings. But it's not rare, either. And if their wives ask them whether they have squashed any spices during the day, they usually lie.

Although they may occasionally refuse to squash spices, French chefs know that if the seasonings are not corrected, they will go astray, and an astray seasoning is a wrong seasoning. Everyone agrees that when seasonings are wrong, they are all wrong.

There is no such thing as slightly wrong seasonings or partly wrong seasonings, unless there is only one seasoning under affliction, in which case it is a problem of singular or plural, and the only chef in history capable of producing a masterpiece with only one seasoning was Maurice de Montenay, who on a Sunday outing near Bastille Day produced an unforgettable Roast Crown Chop of Mutton by baking the chop between two 3-inch layers of licorice.

Corrected seasonings are important because, if the seasonings are not right, they will muddle off in a corner, or discolor, or even abbreviate. It can, for example, be syntactically very troublesome if the seasonings in an alphabet soup are wrong, for then they misspell altogether, and the letters will not pronounce. Indeed, the most persuasive disaster of all fell upon the luckless French Premier of 1944 at a dinner party he gave in Vichy. The alphabet soup seasonings were wrong, and when the soup arrived at the table under its own steam, it was discovered with a scarcely sealed delight that the letters favored Lili Marlene and carried a German postmark.

Anyone seeking the last word on the relativity of spices and absolutism in food might do no better than the honest that was later scriven on the facade of Les Invalides, the home of the Tomb of the Unknown Soldier, who was in fact the irrepressible and inexhumable Napoleon Bonaparte, who, had he had a greater love of stylish hats, could have been pope. There, in letters equal to none but each other, is the fabled, *Duo non, duo sic',* so fabled it is sometimes written aloud. It translates, "Two Wrongs Don't Make a Right," which is now widely disbelieved.

This saying has been promoted ever since Napoleon, leaving behind only his nose and his strut for a brief and unsuccessful transplant, was raised body-first into heaven. It is meant to gladden all our hearts to know that Napoleon sits on the right hand of all seasonings, for it suggests that France is heaven, or else heaven is thoroughly French. In either place, it can help prove to the perfection of doubt whether taste buds are the pathway to immortality.

XXIV

Cooking from Books

Perhaps the rapidly increasing population of French food nuts is due to the fact that food is fun. Of course, as John Edwards has reminded us, there is fun, and then there is *fun*, but this may only explain why he never wrote a cookbook. The French are the ones who deserve most of the credit for putting the fun back into food. This is no accident; the French do not have accidents because France is far too small a country. There is only one preclusion left. In French food, the fun is almost all on purpose.

Like civilized people everywhere, the French have their fun in stages. They do not have their fun all at once, like a purge. They do not put all their fun into a very select group of foods that might inspire the sort of comment, "Oh God, but I really do think a plover is a fun food."

No, the French secret is that they steep themselves slowly in fun, starting with an askance, and then a double-take, and then a lip-curl, and then an eyebrow arch, and then a pair of flared nostrils, and then a heh, and another heh, and then the ha, and then the ha ha, and the triple ha, with a ho, or a double ho, or a hee, or a hee, hee, or a hee[3], and on down the pancreas and into the epidemic, shaking the whole works. If you have to wait an excruciatingly long time for the French to have all their fun, it is certainly worth their wait.

The usual assumption is that the French only have any fast food fun when they blitz the fridge and goozle themselves into an old-fashioned food drunk. This is both a curdled and a rigor mortis, and is hereby laid to rest forever. The honest truth, which can be distinguished from the dishonest truth by the gullibility of the receiver, is that the first tickle in French food fun is ready and waiting in any of the classic recipes, and it erupts the moment you start reading, for you instantly realize that the basic laugh in classic French recipes is that they have no ending.

Examples of unfinished recipes are procreate. Several of the best are found among the classics first published in Mother de Beaurepaire's Cooking for Fun But Mostly for Profit Cookbook, which has now been translated from the French into seventeen languages and five major dialogues. These recipes carry you to the door of the oven and then leave you there to test your mettle for yourself, or they get you half-way through the beating or a third of the way through a beautiful basting, and then, when you turn the page, you find you are left to beat and baste for yourself.

The recipes of the classic French cuisine, therefore, represent a unique style of cooking that is as ingenious as it is disarming. This style has all the charm of an author who leaves the final chapter of her murder-mystery a blank, and it has the same *joie de finir*, or "joyous kissoff", that Amy Winehouse used whenever she tabled a tragedy by living it.

This fun, or "unfinished", approach to the preparation of food has its margin of error. Even a minor misstep, or an almost perfect guess, can lead to tragic endings, as when a turkey Florentine suddenly dismembers into an omelette of cranberries, or when a *gateau de noix* (a rich sort of cake heavily laden with noix) rises well past its bedtime into a sleepy soufflé.

Nevertheless, the challenge of finishing on your own terms what is well begun on someone else's terms, which is very French, is an energetic, for it lets any cook test under fire her analytical glands, his powers of elevation, her innards, and his outbasket.

In short, this is the "Have You Tasted My Finale?" school of food creation, with so many rules and so much artistry that French cooking has become a sort of *lycée* at home, in which every kitchen is a schoolhouse and every student cook gets to eat the daily quiz. Some would call the unfinished recipe France's most enviable response to the possibilities of extension education.

Certainly the most distinctive educational tool developed since the average French kitchen was converted into a *lycée-at-home* is the *'analyse de texte'*, or the analysis of the printed word. Originally a classroom game, and now excluded to the kitchen, the *analyse de texte* actually refers – with that abundant solemnity the French often bring to the fun in food – to the careful use of a cookbook.

Indeed, so important has the *analyse* become in the popularization of French cuisine that anyone who enrolls at the Ecole Cordon Bleu Trois Chefs – one flight up, three doors to the right, and wear a toque – is required to spend the first thirty lessons learning to decipher a serious cookbook while preserving its laughability.

Though the dynamics of the *analyse de texte* need not be detained here, it should be said that it is an effective method for keeping the aspiring cook from learning anything at all about cooking until he has penetrated the wonders of the French paragraph.

There are, of course, many cookbooks to keep the fun alive and well among the citizens of France. Chief of them, as we have pre-mentioned, is the corpulent Larousse Gastronomique. The Larousse's most enviable characteristic is that it is just about equal in weight to the average French chef. This is a cookbook, therefore, never sold closed, for opening it has been the sole cause of death for several members of the cast of Le Misanthrope.

Indeed, lifting the Larousse is said to have permanently suppressed the waist of the great filmmaker Philippe de Broca. It is consequently sold open, propped up in a wheelbarrow, and it can be wheeled away from a French bookstore in approximately part of the time it took "Over the Rainbow" to transition from a musical showstopper to the role of National Anthem of the United States.

It follows as right the might that the most illustrious dowries in all France are those graced by the presence of the family Larousse. Happy is the bride who inherits the treasure, and since the average inherited Larousse has only 93 more monthly payments due on it when it arrives at the bride's door in a dowrybarrow, she can look forward to getting years of credit for her cooking. But she can also use her Larousse in other ways, for publishers of French cookbooks, in their efforts to relate the historic value of the cookbook to the taste of the recipe, always pre-grease the pages.

This gives the entire magnum opus the look and the perfume of ancient parchment, which adds at least two generations of respectability to the family that has it, without in any way making the food taste older, and turns the pages a rich chestnut brown, so that a dowried Larousse becomes not only the perfect bric-a-brac atop the oriental inlay table in the library corner, but also the catalyst of library cookeries all over France.

No matter what the brand name, every cookbook written for the classic cuisine includes a set of instructional symbols so elaborate that every page looks like a sheet of papyrus from the tomb of "Two Tank" Hammon, the artillery hero. The symbols are artistic as well as summary, and a second set of thirty lessons at the Ecole Cordon Bleu Trois Chefs is consequently devoted to their interpretation and imitation, and is conducted under the auspices of the rare book and manuscripts division of the Egyptology Section of the Louvre.

A few of these symbols, some of them in peccable taste, will illustrate the handiwork of their instruction. For example, the symbol of a first finger pointed means in French "Why not try a little more lettuce next to the bone?" while in English it means "Keep an eye on your measuring cups while you're ladling in the flavor," and in American "Go back to the beginning, dummy, it tastes awful so far." The symbol of a bottle means in French, "Pour in just a little dry white wine and let it coddle the eggs without surface bruising until the yellow matches the hair of the Venus de Milo and the white is the white of the white rabbit being hunted close to Aix-en-Ville."

Another symbol, the raised thumb means in German "Anyone who tries to use a Riesling at this point deserves to be living on the other side of the Rhine" while in American it means "Better take a big gulp, honey, you are going to need it to get through this one."

On the other hand, the symbol of a raised center finger (if you count from the right) means in French, "Aha! Now turn it over and carefully sprinkle the cardamom, then cover it with celery leaves and be sure you've got enough wood in your stove." In Italian it means "I don't care how many vermicelli you want to add, this is *pastry*." And in American, "By Christ, I'm going to take that turkey by surprise this time!"

There are, of course, more specific symbols reserved for use in special recipes. They are passed on from generation to generation, sometimes even in abbreviated form. Thus the symbol of two hands having ten fingers in the *Salade Niçoise* recipe means "Don't forget to oil your hands before you grab the hearts of palm" or in Italian, "*Ten* peas, you meatball!" It then turns into two hands showing only thumbs, meaning "No, no, toss it up, up!" and finally the symbol of a right hand with half-fingers, meaning "The really smart cook has his beans sliced at the greengrocer's for a small extra charge."

But if you see the symbol of ten fingers alone in the classic recipe for Brown butter poached in black pears, *Beurre Brun aux Poires Noires*, the symbol means that you must test the heat of the butter after ten minutes by sticking your fingertips into the bubbles at the edge of the pan. If the bubbles break, it is time to pour the butter into the pears' center gravities. If they do not break, you are either using a chintzy Spanish butter or else you forgot to take your mittens off.

Incidentally, if the bubbles have not broken after the first hour of poaching, turn them over and let them cook on the other side. This will stretch the bubbles' membrane and render them more easily breakable. Under no circumstances should you allow the bubbles to go unbroken after two hours, since by this time the pears will have shrunk to the dimensions of an otter's gizzard, and the butter itself will, with a heavy sigh, have converted to oleomargarine.

XXV

On Measurements and Measuring

rench measurements will at first sight stagger the American cook, but will at second sight only seem to stagger. By the third sight, if the American is not fully staggered, she will at least be less fully staggered. (Staggered cooks, incidentally, contrary to the song, do not of themselves spoil the broth, though it has been said they do swallow the sauce.) The first and serious secret in undoing the mystery of French measurements is to say them aloud. This will fortify the ego and make your breath feel benevolent.

For example, a thumbnail of brandy is exactly that. First, say it aloud: "A Thumbnail of Brandy." Then turn the brandy bottle upside down, with the cork still in it. Stand over the bathtub, or some yearning crevasse like the bed pan, unplug the bottle, and hold the thumb under the free-flowing brandy. The brandy must definitely be allowed to run freely onto and across the thumb. (If this were not the indicated method, the directions would not have called for a thumbful of brandy.) If pouring over a bathtub, be sure you have plugged the bathtub, as you will want to collect the rest of the brandy for use in recipes that call for *tubbed* brandy. Or if over a bedpan, then *panned* brandy, etc.

The average American cook is supplied with the regulation cup measure broken down by halves, quarters, and thirds, and with a tablespoon broken down into teaspoons, a half, the quarter, etc. These are generally enough to suffice. But the French metric system is different from ours, and this must be considered in translating the measurements from a French recipe into an American kitchen. The French metric system is based on two very simple principles. The first is that the French kitchen is smaller than the American kitchen. The second is that the French like to get more for their money.

Bear these in mind, and changing over from the French metric to the American metric will be a much more pleasant experience for you. Above all, be advised that the French cup is smaller, though not much smaller, than the American cup, even in brassieres. If, for example, you are cooking in American and are asked to pour a cup of sugar into a spinach mold, first take off the mold. But if you are cooking in French, you must use the French cup.

All you need do is press the top and the bottom of your tongue on top of an American cup of sugar. The amount that sticks to your tongue reduces the original American cup to the exact amount of a French cup, unless, unhappily, you are cursed with the "dwarf" tongue so common in dwarfs, or the "tied" tongue so common among Wall Street titans appearing in front of a Congressional Committee.

To test your tongue for capacity, roll it along the inside of your gums playfully until a tse-tse fly darts by, then spit the fly to death very suddenly. If you succeed, your tongue is at full capacity. If you fail, have your lungs tested for depth, since you will need deep lungs when we get to that French specialty, Deep Lung Soufflé, in which you do the work of the oven.

The French tablespoon is an anomaly, and is larger than the American tablespoon, probably because French tables tend to be smaller. To correct the measurement, hold the full French tablespoon in the left hand, and hold an American quarter-teaspoon in the right hand. Leaning close to the left tablespoon, blow clockwise slowly but steadily, the lips pursed as in parsimony, so that the contents of the left are partially lifted into the quarter-teaspoon on the right.

When the quarter-teaspoon is full, you have a corrected tablespoon in your left hand, and you can store the contents of the right, or quarter-teaspoon, in your Tupperware jar or on the tongue of a particularly lazy house pet, such as a chameleon or a pussy-willow. The same general procedure is followed to get a corrected teaspoon, except here you blow just enough so that the 't' of the left teaspoon is removed, leaving intact the 'ea' so essential to the flavor, and you have the corrected American teaspoon. You can then add the 't' in your right hand to your vocabulary, or to one of your least embellished diphthongs.

XXVI

A Helpless Hint in the Hand

This is the mid-way point along the route of Helpless Hints, a point that straddles both the helpless and the hints. It seems a dandy and a knocker to introduce here a classic French recipe in order to illustrate the kinds of helplessness these hints are all so addicted to adduce. A brief survey of the haute cuisine has revealed that, of all the great recipes at large in la belle France, surely one of the steadfasts is the *'croix de guerre'*, which is the French food equivalent of the Medal of Honor.

The *croix de guerre* is an adaptation of the smaller *croix*, or the even smaller *croisette*, that was pinned to the breast of a female traitor so as to indicate to her tailor the location of the duck grease that had splounced off the business end of the nether lip that formed one of a pair of two nether lips,- the latter being less nether than the former, but nether nevertheless, - that belonged to an Orangeman from the House of Belfast, a youth of distinguished salivation whose every word to the traitor literally floated off his tongue, accompanied on numerous occasions by whatever else was floating on his tongue at the time, like duck grease.

The *croisette* was a handy item, in that it signaled the tailor's area of primal interest, while at the same time soaking up part of the duck grease itself, and thus it served the three muses of all contemporary art: decoration, utility and edibility.

From its humble start at the edge of a disloyal breast, the *croisette* grew to a *croix*, and then, after some of the usual warfare, to a *croix de guerre*. The *croix de guerre* has sometimes been confused with the cross of Lorraine, and this is as good a time as any to assure the world that the two have never had anything serious to do with each other.

The cross of Lorraine is in fact a leghold popular among modern female wrestlers, adopted in toto from the amazingly diversified liturgy of Lorraine Lachaise, whose worship of men in general, and any man in particular, urged her to adopt many surprising ways to continue that worship once it had begun.

It was often said, though in a low whisper, for those whose ears were lower than usual, that a night of worship in Lorraine's company could easily endure throughout the day following, if and when she decided to surmount you with the cross of Lorraine. But for those who know that the *croix de guerre* is not the cross of Lorraine, and who are saying to themselves with a big smug, "Aha, so it must be that military décor!" this is almost the perfect time for us to declare that the *croix de guerre* is *not* any kind of military decoration, nor is it the 'x' drawn in ink on the shirt of a prisoner of war found consorting with other prisoners of war in a manner conducive to the arrest of hygiene.

The uses to which this particular *croix* (as it is popularly called by the populars in France) has been put are mythical. It was put to the torch by Muslims under the command of Osama bin Quaddafi so that he could read his graffiti by night. It was deployed in fitful rows to stop a tank attack at the Battle of Tours in 1679. It was used by thousands of French fathers who, in desperation to rid themselves of their marriageable daughters, tied a *croix* to their thighs as an edible come-all-ye.

But the earliest known use of the *croix* was that employed by sixteenth-century movie censors. Full of the smiles that always accompany a stockpile of censored moments, the censors carried packets of *croix* around with them in order to festoon the only parts of the movie that ever proved exciting.

It is a sign of the times that anyone trying to create this famous dish within the confines of a theological seminary should wear a pith helmet. Such caution accords with that hidebound legality often espoused by the American law firm Rigby, Rugby, Spoonbill and Ragoon: "Self-protection is 99% of the law."

This was even more so when the ageless and recently deceased theosopher, Rhinegold Dragonette, whose handmaiden Jessica was for over thirty years R. Wagner's leading underwater contralto, once warned a brace of Canadian hockey players they could not skate away from the dangers of a *croix*. When challenged to prove that statement, with all its obligato, Rhinegold wisely responded that even hockey players must comprehend that it is easier to pass a camel through the eye of a needle than to pass by the Almighty on your way into the oven.

The *croix* is a baked good. It is made of a very special dough culled from the willies of Aunt Jemima. The delectable advantage of this kind of dough is that it can be made successfully on almost any day of the year, sun in, sun out. But it is perhaps not wise to try to make it on a day when one of the superpowers is sending another rocketship into outer space, for this shakes the willies out of the dough and causes its glands to excrete excitement.

Such excitement makes for a highly uneven result, tending to cause surface eruptions not unlike lunar craters. Nor should it be tried on any day when the pollution count is above four, since the dough will inflate to a gray color like silly putty and will bake very peevishly, coughing all the while, and must then be shrouded with a layer of gauze so as to ease the congestion.

Lighting the right stove for a *croix* is a challenge even to the accomplished arsonist, but it is the kind of small elegance that leads so many French gourmets into funny farms ere they are middle-aged. The stove Charles de Gaulle used when arriving tourist class in France just after the blossom of the War of the Roses is the stove that has been approved for baking the authentic *croix*. It is of course a wood-burning stove, with yellow cheeks and a superb memory, so be careful what you say in the kitchen.

The French wood-burning stove has a strong preference for garlic wood and will give years of extra service for free if this minor vice is steadily indulged. A note of caution, however. After it has digested a rack of garlic wood, it tends to slight attacks of melodiously inarticulate hiccups. These can affect whatever is baking by urging it into a different shape.

Therefore do not bake anything in the stove for at least two hours after it has taken its garlic wood. And when you first open the oven door after it has finished the wood, stand to one side and face out into the room, exhaling constantly for about three minutes or until your nasal passage clogs up in self-defense. The stove is now ready.

If the floor is wooden, so much the better. If the floor is linoleum, take a hollow-handled knife, fill the handle with a light celery paste, and cut a two-foot-square section out of the linoleum and lift it gently, tapering the glue off the bottom with the skewer from your shish kebab. (If you are baking in a neighbor's home, which is bound to be nearby, you can ignore altogether the shish kebab skewer, as it is hard to pronounce and is violently pro-Middle East.)

Placing the linoleum in front of the stove, kneel down promptly before you forget, with both knees touching the floor simultaneously, and rest there until the knees are flush with the floor. Scrape your knees together for about two minutes Eastern Standard Time, or until the pain is particularly acute in the area of your taste buds. This friction will slowly but very gently singe your pubic hair to an erudite shade of Moroccan walnut, a flattering counterpoint to the African indigo of your abdomen, unless, of course, you are an albino.

You will notice a sudden spray of sparks leaping out from between your knees and vaulting around the kitchen as hotly as Ryan Seacrest himself vaults when proddingly goosed by that unsuspected sister of the Prince of Wales, the Princess of Wales. Grab these sparks in the order of their appearance, being as careful of their hierarchy as was P.T. Barnum when he put the blind trapeze artists on after the main stripper. Then line the sparks up along the index finger, where you can keep them warm by covering them temporarily with your very best wishes.

Stare but obliquely at the *croix*. Keeping your hand amiss so as not to disturb the sparks, resurrect your tongue from the helplessness it endures while lying on its side recuperating from a season of afterthoughts, and curl it into the shape of a rolled pancake, or, if you are of an Italian extract, into a canoli. Then vibrate the glottis in cadence with the glow of your vocabulary so that the underside of the breath collects inside the curl of the tongue.

When the glottis is striking G at the base of its clef and the tongue is exuding a B sharp on the half-note, release the tongue directly at the point where the index finger leaves the palm of the hand. This sharp burst of song-filled air will carry the sparks off the finger and across into the oven, which, with any luck, they will find even warmer than the finger they so recently left.

This ritual, while tedious in appearance, is designed by oven manufacturers to convince you to rid yourself of your wood-burning stove. However, it has the advantage of charring your floor to the specifications of the 18th century Idaho farmhouses recently favored by the better Home Design magazines. This ritual lends to the house the air of excitement that always accompanies an acrid fire; it will bring your neighbors on the hoof, and they will form a ring-around-the-rosie, singing "Ashes, ashes, all fall down."

This sort of frolic adds to the entire scene a carnival atmosphere, and to the *croix* a flush of victory that adds so much to its popularity, something like the gorgeous Brigitte Bardot, known to projectors all over the world as BB, must have felt when she discovered, after nine sex-mongering years of stripping her soul bare for French cinerealistes, that she was in fact Bernard Berenson.

If the pollution count goes above nine while the *croix* baking is in process, attention must be paid to the danger. The easiest – and the right - thing to do is to call the Weather Bureau and announce that there has been a mistake, and that the pollution count is actually just under three.

If you speak authoritatively and elocutionally, mouthing the whole digits as firmly as your dentures will allow, and grasping the phone firmly in your right hand and wiping your mouth with a sprightly cheer, the Bureau should cooperate and lower the official reading. It may be an outright lie, but it creates that spirit of accommodation in which the *croix* dough thrives, and you are assured that it can go on baking happily, as if there were no death count in pollution outdoors.

One or two final notes will end our notes on the *croix de guerre*. It is vitally important that you do not bake a *croix* on a day when you have carried a heavy handbag or briefcase, as this extends the arm and weakens the muscles, and when you knead the dough after carrying something heavy, the dough is as uneven as the relationship between an addict and his parole officer. When it is baked in such circumstances, it rises much more fully on one side than the other, like a woman with a semi-inflatable bra, causing acute self-embarrassment.

So if, in an effort to placate, you favor the *croix* with one of those smiles a federal bureaucrat reserves for the employee whose position is being "selected out" on the following day, the *croix* will probably reward you by sentencing you to years of servitude in plenipotentiary. In short, the *croix* has its own standards, which is a tradition long favored by the French.

The final thing that distinguishes this creation from most other French food is that you are not always obliged to kill something or someone as the first step in its preparation. It should however be prepared in the shade, or at the very least you should have someone stand over your shoulder during the last five minutes and lightly flour a 40-watt light bulb for you to stand beneath. Of course, if you hesitate too long, you will lose your hesitation, for, as the ancients so often said, in tongues unbeknownst to themselves and lately translated otherwise, "A penny for your hesitation."

If you have lost, and the *croix* comes out of the oven cranky and dishevelled, with a slight acne, then you lose, and you must go directly to Jail without passing Go or collecting your wits. But you must resist killing whatever it was you had avoided killing before, or its nearest eligible, depending on the specifications of the recipe.

This latter decision, this scared reluctance, is called the *'coupe de résistance.'* It is short for the French expression that became popular in the student wars of 1968 when it was flung from the barricades: *"Une coupe de résistance vaut une pièce de grâce!"* ("Even a tiny bit of resistance deserves a joint.")

XXVII

On the Bottle

Wine is an almost exhaustible subject, and just talking about it can stain the teeth. Yet it has inspired many millions of people, from the very highest boozers to the lowest drunks. The secret of its essence is found in the old French proverb: "A diamond is for wow, but a grape is forever."

There are a few ne'er-do-wells who consider a grape nothing more than a raisin with complexion glow, but the true suppliants, the ones who refuse to milk their cows in non-vintage years, call upon wine as the lotion of the conscience and the lubricant of the genitals. They strike the harp and join the chorus that wine, in its own place and with the right food, is nowhere else, and it never was.

French wine comes in an assortment of colors and flavors that are easy to learn and likely to remember, and serve the added purpose of helping us to distinguish a good French wine from high-purpose vinegar, coconut oil, or any of the lesser mendicaments. The current three top flavors are, in the order of their appearance, Bordeaux, Burgundy and Champagne, although it is said that, when it comes to Champagne, the French have beer pocketbooks.

This is the same top trinity that fans of Caesar's Gallic Wars will recall from the opening volley in chapter one, when J. Caesar, in a widely imitated throwaway, cast his dice upon the waters of the Satyricon and watched them sink ironically. "All Gaul," he said, "is divided into three wines." And so saying, he slung a grape around his neck for its medicinal value and drank his way into battle.

One of the reasons for the international celebrity of French wines is that they are so well known for being well known. No matter how good they taste, or how bad, everyone knows French wines are very good, and everybody likes to be able to relax into a good wine, knowing they may be the victims of the most benign propaganda in the world, but mercifully pervious to it.

The Dadaists, and those who follow parental hormones, have helped the world accept the vicissitudes of French wine illusion ("l'illusion du vin") by promoting that a good wine deflates the tonsils, an indifferent wine discolors the tongue, an excellent wine robs the rich to ply their piper, but a superb wine flexes forevermore the clavicle of the diva, allowing her to deasperate her thrills as she wills.

French wine first came into prominence at the top of a hill in the year 23 A.D., and has not descended since. It happened that a host of Hannibal's elephants were picking their way through the Alps in quiet retreat from the Pope's anticipations. Slung about their forenecks were large wooden casks of Boave Solla, a derelict chianti then being arbored in the far platitudes of Umbria. As they crested an especially steep incline, the elephants got thirsty. They refused snow, and had to be given draughts from their own totes.

It was a mighty thirst, mightily quenched, and before the guards could shout, "What ho!" or "Belay the elephants!" a sudden herd of inebriates swarmed down the Alps onto French soil, waving their trunks. It was a sight that was enough to inflame the thorax of many the watching farmers. For several years, the herd wandered all across France, scaring chickens and desecrating crops, and the hapless farmers realized they were encumbered.

But one of their leaders, Jacques Tutot, himself a pragmatic, noticed that the elephants were having more babies the longer they stayed on French soil, and assumed that, if he could purchase a few vats of Boave Solla from the Umbrians, he could besot the herd to the point of pink and pipe them right out of France. He asked the Umbrians for help, but they were so delighted at the general French discomfort that they sent them nothing more than a trunkful of sympathy, though they had been asked for a snootful of Solla.

But Jacques was an entrepreneur and a good scout. He stole into Umbria and out, carrying with him two gallons of Boave roots. In the following weeks, on the hills around his farm at Prix d'Italie, his neighbors watched him planting the roots. They said to each other, "It is a thrill to watch the man who tills the soil to grow the wines to harvest the grapes to press them flat to spill the juice to fill the vats that stand in the cave that Jacques built."

Then he took the best of his grapes and he rented them out to his neighbors at huge stud fees, and in three seasons the area winos had suppressed enough juice to requench the thirsting herd.

All year long they offered tubs of their Boave Solla to the elephants, who adored the stuff. In two years their trunks were vermilion, and, by the end of the third year, the procreates had again become inebriates. Then Jacques put them at parade rest, and to the gaze of his countrymen led a very long line of pink elephants home to Algeria to dry out.

And so grew the Boave Solla grapes of France, through centuries of pith and panic, until that period in the development of French appliances when the wine-burning stove became the enameled darling of provender. Since domestic wine had to be used for all general-purpose heating and daily cooking, the quantity of wine became more important than its quality, and wine merchants, or winos, prospered.[6]

Yards of vines grew to kilometers, and French kitchens resounded with the demand, "Throw more Richebourg '93 in the stove, it's time to cook the pork loins." From Bordeaux and Burgundy, from Tavel and Rosé echoed the messages: "Buy Chateau Montrose '79, it burns much longer", or "Try Pétrus-Picque '14, for a cleaner, more comfortable smoke."

The French were not completely satisfied with having enough wine to keep their stoves burning. They wanted something fancier, a wine that would be the hallmark of their calling card, so that when company was coming for breakfast or the weekend, everyone would know the French cared enough to pour the very best. Lacking any especially colorful local wine flavor, they imported from Oberammergau some serious sabbatical wines. From Italy came unwed Valpolicellas swathed in rattan, and from Germany came Moselles glazed from the banks of the Piper-Pepsick.

To the general sorrow, these imports were not very notable wines. They therefore consulted the entrails of a greyhound, and learned that they needed god's help, so they invited Vulcan to change her affiliations and improve her image by becoming

---

6 The winos are not to be completely confused by unflattering references to the shipwrecks scattered along the Bowery. They are pronounced "shipwrecks" with a hard final K, and a sibilant 's', whereas the winos are pronounced with a soft W, as is the final 'w' in "titwillow".

a wine god. Vulcan was so delighted she shut down Mt. Aetna for two years, and in her acceptance speech she promised that French wines would soon be into the vat and out of the fire.

This was news indeed, and the hopeful French went out to stare at the drupaceous wines in the grape yards, thinking of the outsize banding tree, and they dreamed of soon having their own superior vintages.

Ever since she had been a baby god, Vulcan had always said that she would only help those who helped themselves. She therefore immediately enlisted the aid of the French winos in finding a vintage wine. The winos told her they had three or four problems to contend. The first was that they did not like being called winos. She asked them whether they were such cretins as to think she liked being called Vulcan, and they said, "But you are no longer a baby god, so change your name if you wish."

The suggestion was unadorned, and lifted poor Vulcan right off her cloud. "And what would I call myself?" she asked quick as a lightning trig. "Go by the sound of it," they said. "If it sounds nice, you can get away with anything!" "Well, I shall go to the Acropolis for a while and ask my father, mighty Mars the Orbited, and my mother, Queen Andromeda the Strained, for a new name." And laying her finger straight into her nose, she huffed and she puffed and to heaven she rose.

This was no help at all to the poor winos. So, following the minim that, if you want to get some action, you go straight to the top, they purchased the King's ear for an evening and bought a law that forbade anyone from addressing or referring to a wino as a wino, but thereafter only as a *négociant* – not so much because they negotiated the juice out of the grape, or the wine out of the bottle, but the franc out of the pocket.

With dignity intact, the *négociants* turned to their second problem. They knew that so long as the wine-burning stove persisted, they would either have to continue bottling wine hot and selling it beneath asbestos corks, or sell it cold and intensify their nationwide campaign for a hotter French tongue. They hit on a clever solution.

By the simple expungent of declaring publicly that burning wine gives off an odor that both irrigates the liver and disarms the tourist trade, the *négociants* changed overnight a nation's appliance, and when the chief *négociant* of Sauternes, Emile Rieussec, stood atop the Sacré Coeur with a megaphone in his larynx and asked aloud, "Is Paris burning?" hundreds of thousands of French homeowners switched to coal.

An appreciative nation captured in verse a poem with which they serenaded the demise of the wine-burning stove and the victory of the *négociants*. If it seems without rhyme, and with reason, the lyric must be read at full tilt and sung with full lilt, though it can be easily derived from a flagging memory, and so it goes:

A grape a day is a Chardonnay,
Two grape a day, the famed Gamay,
Three grape a day worth two a day,
Two grape a day worth one Gamay,
One grape a day a half-Chardonnay,
Half-Chardonnay better they say,
Than no Gamay or one a day.[7]

The *négociants* gained from their victory such a hanced appreciation of their own economic influence that, in a torrent of self-genuflection, they decided thereafter to call their homes by such special names as 'chateaux' or 'domiciles' or even the lofty 'caves', and to the present day the message on a wine label, "*Mise en bouteilles dans nos caves,*" in a translation that

---

7 The exclusion from the poem of the Pinot Purpre, or the Purple Pinot, that gamacious grape named for the Hellenic eyeball of the same disposition, went unmissed by the Purple Pinot eaters, and it was sorely unmissed.

favors length over the breath, declares that this wine was bottled inside the house of one of those *négociants* who were responsible for permanently extinguishing the wine-burning stove.

Having grown in their respectability, the happy-go-luckless *négociants* were ready to press on with their search for the great French wine, for they believed that, should they take arms against a vat of bubbles and by their end uphold them, sooner or later something magical would spill over, and they would be there to snare it. They waited for years, their throats parched, their labels unglued. They tried growing their grapes at night, but it only resulted in a wine that was much darker and could not take the air as long as daylight wine, though it certainly blinked less often.

They tried to round out the flavor by squaring the roots, but the results were square grapes, harder to press, tight at the corners, and even a little cubic. They tried frolicking in the arbor every day, sprinkling the wines with attar of afterglow and her-bessence of mangrove, but the wines broke out in a rash and had to be rubbed down four times daily with calamine. In effect, everything they tried was out of effect.

And every year the Grand Sommelier of France, whose nose was worse than his bite and who could smell two entire rooms and an alcove in a single inhaling and still leave one nostril underhaled, would descend from Paris in an entourage of cups, and ere he began his long list of swallows, he would clear the cobwcbs off his vocal chords with a sudden snort of high-caliber turpentine, and only then would he take a sniff and a glut of each wine sample brought to him.

Then, looking out over the herds of stamping feet, his cups tonking together in the wind like tinkers' damns, his eyes apop with the surprise of a descendant of early American colonists being patronized by a second-generation out of St. Louis, he would declare the yearly verdict: "*Jus de tomate! C'est pas possible!*" (or) "It sure doesn't taste like tomato juice!"

In the year 1854, however, during an argument over the relative merits of the bespoke truffle and the unsung truffle, later resolved in favor of the theretofore unsung bubble truffle – which, when it boiled right down to it, toiled in the cauldron on only half the soil and with double the bubble – the assembled *négociants* realized that any final decision on the quality of French wines was theirs to make, and theirs alone.

And so they set to work drafting the rules for a nationwide contest on the model of the then-famous Miss America pageant, with this exception, that the shape of the container was not to be confused with the tastiness of the product. They summoned their samples from hither, thither, dither, and yon, and in what historians have designated the longest successful wine drunk in the nation's history, spent all of 1855 sampling, registering, and voting on all the wines of France.

The results of the balloting, since known as the Classification of 1855, rank the 1200 assorted French vintages according to weight, volume, taste, and label. No extra points were given for baroque seals or musical corks, but many a vintage ended up being classified according to the secrecy with which the *négociants* would provide each other with handmaidens to help them take their tongues off their work. This was in accordance with the dictum of Abelard*, who said, "Behold the maidens with their hoods in hand. Methinks small maids in hoods make light hands and short work."

As it turned out, the wines being ranked were the 1854 harvest, soon discovered to be less than the taste sensation of the nation. One knowledgeable tourist from Greater Western New York even likened the average 1854 vintage to a quart of Hudson River water, while another from the same name found that the

---

* Said Heloise to her sister nuns: "Any dictum of Abelard's is my dictum, and if you don't like it, you can go screw yourselves."

best of the lot could easily compete with the treacle from the nose of St. Therese Delicieux.

The results of the classification contest were published everywhere, and a hypothermal ballyhoo arose all over France, since the very existence of such a contest had already implied that there was something worth competing for, that there were worthy contestants, and that someone was lucky enough to possess the reigning tastebuds in the choice of winners.

The contemporary reader will recognize in these solemn provisos the same rules by which the Miss America decathlon is run, an Olympic in which a jury of the undersexed and the overaged, whose average association with the product at hand is still long overdue, manages to select a winner from the herd. In the case of Miss A., she is a kewpie presumed to represent the average American female of the late teens because she has the vibrant sexuality of Richard Simmons and the depth of Miss Lohan, and so can be expected to marry, as her just dessert, the Sam of the Uncle Sam poster family.

After months of red and white tongues, the judges concluded it was possible to distinguish at least four major categories. A wine could be a *'hors classe'*, a *'cru exceptionelle'*, a *'cru supérieur'*, or a *'cru ordinaire'*. Those who are strangers to the classifications, or to their own tongues, will find these classifications as luminously clear as a horoscope by Sidney Hubble of Hubble telescopic fame. The following descriptions of the grosser categories, or 'classifications grosses', will be instructive, especially since they are now memorized by every third-grade French schoolchild as a necessary preamble to the greater understanding of Aubrey Beardsley's drawings:

> ***Hors classe:*** a cheap, almost tawdry, and usually masculine wine, easily procured and often beneath contempt; the price is very high, the pleasure comes to an early climax, and

an unpleasant, grapey taste is often left in the mouth and other human oracles.

Cru exceptionelle: a wine that is vatted, dyed, and bottled by an exceptional work gang; a *cru exceptionelle* sometimes suggests that the grapes have been overhandled, even pawed and sometimes leave distinguishable, if not identifiable, fingerprints on the back of the biscuspids and on the upper tongue. An *exceptionelle* is, in a good year, better than usual, and yet immediately priced for recall, since it has a conscious accent and a parlor demeanor. Albert de Gorgonzola calls it out loud, but it is still a wine that has been befriended, if not compromised.

Grand cru: a grand *cru*, like Chateau Lettuce or Putrachet-Gamin, is a wine well on its way to the greatness of a *vin ordinaire*, though it does not always travel well. A grand *cru* reminds the distasteful memory that a grape can be squeezed without being squashed. When rolled over the tongue, a grand *cru* flattens the teeth and enhances the arch of the mouth roof. It is marked by a high in titanic acid, giving the wine a buoyancy that endures until it collides with ice cubes, and is noted for the wide absence of appleseed and other flotsam.

Vin ordinaire: so-called because it looks just like any other wine both outside and in. Such a wine is the darling of the vat and the gild on the lily. With its thick feelings and its golden calf, the *vin ordinaire*, or *'bon cru'*, is the great sleeper of the wine industry and the bouquet of which memorable nosebleeds are made. The annual harvest of the *'ordinaires'* is so limited that quantity is measured in the handsful, and each of them carries its own copyright.

The grapes are handled only by the owner or his designee, and always with his kid's gloves. They are then catapaulted downwards in order to be held affirmatively between the knees, at which the owner sings stanzas from the beloved autumnal carol, *"Entre les genoux a gauche a droite,"* ("Between the knees left to right") which coaxes from the grapes a few authentic tears that are collected, while still sad, in minor vials held by well-attended grooms, and later sold, just as its winter cousin sells the frozen 'ice-wine', as the very precious 'vin de la tristesse.'...the wine of sadness.

While the classification contest was still in full throttle to find or create a motto that would emblazon the proverbs of France for years to come and fill the space at the bottom of restaurant menus in the absence of the likeness of Napoleon Brandy, the *négociants* went straight to the collector of dithyrambs at the Sorbonne, and asked him elegaically whether he had any ancient couplets lying around that could be put to better, more economic use. As one of the suppliants urged, "Our industry for a motto!"

The Sorbonne expert did have a handsome little 16th-century Italian couplet about youth being the sediment in the bowl of life, but this was rejected as being too closely associated with the fall of the House of Bardolino. The *négociants* made it clear that a 14th-century saying would be better, as no one seemed to understand anyone else in any of the 14th-century languages, and so, following the example of telegrams arriving at the CIA, it could be translated in accordance with the wishes of the receiver, which might in fact explain not only why the CIA chose the motto, "It is better to receive than to give," but also why the motto is always found within parentheses, even when spoken, or whenever it is received in code.

An archivist and literator who cannot come up with an appropriate motto for a group of well-meant *négociants* is at heart a bereft, and the scourge of his idols. In terror for his reputation, the Sorbonne man exhumed dozens of mottos, proverbs and captions, ranging in speed from two to ten words, in color from cognac to grape, in meaning from light to dense. They covered such topics as the courage of a prostitute and the use of pastels in flavoring American beef, all of which the *négociants* found timely but irreproachable. In desperation, they turned to Arnold Daudet, who, flexing his tricep each time he sounded a diphthong, agreed to give it a whirl.

Daudet's first attempt at a saying that would combine the national appeal of Audrey Tatou with the rudiments of good stone carving was introduced at a luncheon served aboard a trading ship anchored in the English Channel. It read:

"Every wine under the sun is like a dinner without food."

Diagnostic reactions to this particular rendition were equal in intensity to those that reverberated around Chase National Bank when its customers learned that the new bank policy under serious consideration was to give only a Tupperware juicer to anyone opening a savings account of ten thousand dollars or more, without regard for race, creed, color or political convictions, and especially without regard for the bank's race, creed, color or political convictions. In short, Daudet had failed. His second attempt, for which he had the highest hopes, was this:

"A wine without sun is like food without dinner."

This one was destined for the same lofty niche in the nation's affection once earned by Felix Fortinbras, the leader of the official 1953 French mountain-climbing expedition that assaulted the treacherous slopes of Drums of Death, an Algerian crag once planted to Dutch elms and huckleberry.

The expedition was a tenacious squad, but they plunged to a prematurely conclusive grave when the entire party but Felix, just twelve feet short of the summit, fell the full 50 feet to the very base of the mountain, all because Felix, at the top of the rope, needed something to tie the French flag to his ski pole as a marker, and forgetfully excerpted the necessary length out of the life-line stretching between Him and Climber Two, and his decedents.

The *négociants* were profoundly disappointed that Daudet's mottos had captured neither his own or anyone else's imagination. And so in his third sally he summoned both poetic license and common sense in a couplet that for horizontality would make the Eiffel Tower seen upended:

"Sun in the wine, wino's delight,
Food in the dinner, always at night."

No sooner had he finished this one than Daudet knew it was already an ancient saying. The *négociants*, however, felt it was a little too ancient in meaning and a little too modern in fog, and, paying Daudet for his best intentions, voted to offer a thousand francs to the Association of German *Négociants* for full rights to their second motto, "A meal without wine is like a day without sunlight."

After negotiating a price of two million francs, the Germans accepted the offer, and the motto now competes for the title of Premier Motto of France with two time-honored sayings: "*Honi soit qui mal y pense*", ("Anyone who thinks ill of me can shove it") and "*Aprés le deluge, moi*", ("After the Great Flood, there's me!").

Now that they had a respectable name, a wine classification, and a nationally-known commercial, the *négociants* were three-fourths of the way to dominating the world's wine market. All they needed was some of that old black magic, without the icy fingers up and down the spine – that hand of the fairy god-mother that can transport the ordinary or ordinaries into paradise, like the marriage of a circus and a Cecil B. DeMille, or the tinsel blonde on Madonna, the hiccups in the voice that is bedded down iin Meryl Streep, or the unspeakable sorrow in the eyes of John Boehner.

They had all the necessities except a superb wine, and since they too believed you cannot make a silken sow purse its ear, they eventually recognized that the only answer was to take a wine that enjoyed regularity and surround it with such occult ritualism that a very ordinary bottle of $2 wine, when adorned with ritual, would sell for $27 a bottle, even in a poor dumb place like the Polymer Islands, and even higher in such ritual-starved countries as the United States.

This was hardly unfair. The *négociants* felt that if a face painted on a balloon upped the price by a thousand percent, then a little good-natured dancing about the bottle, combined with a sniff or two of scholarship and a dash of that off-hand reverence professional tennis players reserve for the taped wrist, might just add up to a blend of worship that could command a far prettier penny in the collection plate than taste itself would admit.

And so, turning to that infinite purveyor of symbol and ritual, the Judaeo-Christian heritage handed down to the Gentiles by Gilbert and Sullivan, these uncanny businessmen stole a page from the *missa solemnis* (aka a solemn Mass) and divided the wine ritual into nine parts:

> *The Annunciation:* ("It looks like a perfectly banner year, if only the fog doesn't mildew entirely before it lifts.")
> *The Visitation:* ("Well, thank god for that! Last year when I turned over these wines, all the leaves were stamped 'U. S. Reebok'.") *The Birth:* ("You know, I said to myself, if I let these little tikes stay another minute, well, oh sure, they'd probably get a little fatter, but, well, it just seemed the time had come, right? Oh, you do develop a feel for it...") *The Baptism:* ("I want every single skin sewed back up as soon as the seeds are spitted up. I'm taking no chances. Then we dunk them all together into the olive oil, but just for

a second! Hey, tell those jerks from Capetown to get their tuxedos on quick – we're ready to go to press!")

These are followed by the *First Holy Communion*: ("Je-sus! By the time this Beaujolais is a month old, it is really going to be young!") *The Confirmation*: ("Yes, this Clos de Bèze is aging perfectly. But watch it mid-bottle, and if you start seeing wrinkles, rub it down with Vaseline behind the label and drink it right away. It's always at its full maturity when its sugar has been brought up close to the surface.") *Holy Orders*: ("This is a wine blessed by the Almighty. Don't touch it with a ten foot-pole until it's old enough not to care. A really great wine has got to be a virgin. You can't go around desecrating it with lips!")

These are followed by *Matrimony*: ("I made a deal with Cordier. He's selling me half his red rejects, and I'm mixing them with my white has-beens, and we're calling it Union de Cordier '07, the first of the great French pinks! We figure $18 a bottle right off, and higher West of the Rockies.") *Extreme Unction*: ("Yes, a beautiful life. No, we're not sure one way or the other, so we decided we won't take any chances. Yes, there's still a lot of the old bounce so we'll pray over it. Makes you think back, doesn't it? I remember our first meeting, way back when we were both young and beautiful... Shhh...they're opening the cork...")

Although it is hard to say whether reverence engenders humility, or vice versa, the French have made it possible for the world's population to stand before a French wine and still be on their knees. The secret of any ritual is in its length, of course, for anything or anyone worth our attention is worth a great deal of attention, and the successful ritualist rightfully equates length with respect.

Taking this one step further, the Don't Forget Christ Was a Layman League might claim that Catholic marriages last longer than Protestant and Jewish marriages because the Catholic wedding ceremony lasts three times longer than theirs, but the really important item is this: even a little ritual goes a long way, and ritual has carried French wine from the obscurity of fermenting grape juice to world acclaim as the nectar of the afflicted and the stuff that takes all the wrinkles out of a botox ad.

But, as the more serious practitioners of hara-kiri will tell you, ritual is not the only path to the after-life. The *négociants* of France were not content to envelop their wines in ritual and let it go at that. They sought an effective means to introduce urgency into wine drinking, and thereby raise the price of a bottle by at least five more dollars.

Harkening to that old Mexican pristine, "Time is pesos," the *négociants* decided that the mystery of time would be the secret ingredient in their economic success, and so they proliferated the fiction that any French wine worthy of a foreign throat lasts only an hour or two, and then vanishes into a mere shadow of its former grapes.

This may have been stuff or it may have been nonsense, but it was certainly a direct contradiction of the oenologists at Nimes, whose theory was that a wine had to be open at least a week before one dared approach the bottle, and if anyone tried three lusty inhales of a wine before the necessary week was out he would find his anus had wilted.

But because most people think time is to be swallowed rather than breathed, the *négociants* won, and tradition now has it that the more French wine you drink, the faster you get the time of day. This emphasis on speedy drinking proved as well what we have long suspected – that the evil consequences of wasting time is the easiest thing to sell.

(We are reminded of the ploy the great diamond mine Harry Winston so often used successfully: "Hurry and get your own Hope Diamond before it's too late! Only one to a customer!") More importantly, the rate of French wine consumption went as high as the proverbial proverb. Instead of emptying three glasses in four hours, the average drinker of French wine, with appreciation glands heightened, began gulping down the equivalent of a liter of wine in two hours. The sun of France has smiled warmly on its wine ever since.

❧

XXVIII

On Preparing the Nose for Inhaling

Not every development in the French wine mystique can be attributed to the French. The importance of the nose to the growth of the French economy, for example, which can never be overdistended, is due directly to the Americans who, while not enjoying the same nasal grandeur as the French, nevertheless learn at an early age to make the most of what they have.

Chieftaine among American nosegrowers was the then-anonymous Mrs. James Van Buren, a duncolored beauty who once gave a dinner party in honor of her husband, the ex-president-to-be. It was at this dinner party that a new wine mystique was inaugurated and a new wine expression, "bouquet," was gathered.

Following the nineteenth-century custom, Mrs. Van Buren first served port and then starboard, until her guests were virtually amidships. Then she produced a fully-corked sauvignon Lilly '51 as her *vin-de-siècle*. (This can either mean 'the wine of the century' or 'another wine made out of siecle.') The guests were agape at the thickset lavender bottle set in the middle of a pewter tankard otherwise stocked full of nasturtiums, rosegays, and kumquat blossoms.

After the cork was removed, the tankard was passed around so that the guests could warm their noses with the heat of the wine while protecting the delicate lining of their nostrils with simultaneous sniffs of the flowers, the combination of which caused them to exclaim, "Ah, what a bouquet!"

The demands of protocol eventually required the removal of the flowers to the sideboard when it was discovered that most cabinet ministers present suffered from a palsy of the Eustachean tube that was too easily pollinated and not easily blown away. However, once these and other Americans had gotten accustomed to the smell of wine by itself, they continued to observe the custom. Even today, if one listens carefully, one hears the murmur of "Ah, the bouquet..." everywhere in the world where French wine is drunk, except of course where people take their flowers very seriously.

Like every basically ritualistic commodity, wine is eminently suited to the scrutiny that can be lavished upon it by those educated in the intricacies of its witchcraft. The label is really the face of the wine, and can be read very easily by those schooled in its signals. One of the most important signals is the year. Usually stuck off in a corner, the year refers to the date when the owners of the vineyard finally were able to get a cork into the bottle. The year is terribly important.[8]

---

8 The year 1957, for example is considered one of the greatest years for wine because it was in that year that F. Truffaut began filming *The Four Hundred Blows*. The year 1993 is another immortal year for French wine because that was the year Jerry Lewis burned his hairpiece in effigy on the Rue Tissot, and we all know how the French adore Jerry Lewis.

Another signal is the name. If the name is Pommard, for example, this indicates that the wine is made to resemble apples. A name like Chateauneuf simply means that there is a new owner of the chateau, whereas a Chateauneuf du Pape means the Pope has bought himself another chateau, probably one with vineyards.

Another signal is the word just below the name of the chateau or domicile. *Cuvée*, for example, means the wine has been sifted through a piece of underwear, among which the French have a particular fascination for Fruit of the Loom. But a *Tête de Cuvée* means that a linen-brimmed hat was placed over the forehead of the vat before it was tipped towards the empty bottles.

Other signals are random. The notice '*Mis en bouteilles dans nos caves,*' when found in small initial caps, can mean that a glassblower is employed on the premises as a tourist attraction, and can be found somewhere down in the caves.

Finally, for the full hygienic effect, a red band crossing the label diagonally means that, sometime prior to shipping, the wine was under quarantine, but the quarantine has now been lifted, though strictly as a favor to the people of France. The black border on a label signals that the owner of this particular vineyard has died, though not necessarily of this wine.

XXIX

Decanting Wine

Once a person has learned that reading a wine label is as good as judging a book by its cover, it is high time for a little decanting. To decant a wine means to remove the cant. In its simplest form, decanting a wine means something far simpler than when it is in its simpler form, when it is anything but simple.

The decanting equipment that is absolutely de rigueur in the United States is known as bell, book, and candle. A beeswax candle, vintage 1939, or a regulation candle from every other off-year save one, is the best bet if one is looking for a safe candle year, although lovers of yellowjacket wax will prefer a lighter year, and 1955 is recommended, if you can get it.

The first step in decanting wine is to ring the bell in order to warn your neighbors that you are about to decant so they can turn off their two-way radios. (This also serves to distinguish between your intention of decanting and your interest in defrocking. Defrocking your wine requires a sense of the naughty, and a camera. Note that defrocking is the quicker and more time-consuming procedure, in which the host strips the glass off the wine bottle in front of a picture window while the guests peep in from outside.

Defrocking can be very laborious if the wine is a vintage year, for French wine bottles add a layer of glass every year, and so a superb half-bottle of 1935 Chateau Palmer often grows into a magnum by the 1970's, a phenomenon which induces a guest to thank the host for having saved the largest wine for the last.

A three-step process can be particularly tri-partite for the uninitiated. Though the bell of the decant gives music to soothe the savage wine, and the candle keeps you from burning your bridges at both ends, the real heart of wine decanting is in the selection of the book.

A longtime favorite was *For Whom the Bell Tolls*, but, since its birth in paperback, it has been found to be rather spineless, and so gives uneven results, except when its final chapters have been warmed on Barack Obama's inner spring mattress. For those who prefer the heavy, detailed decant, the *Information Almanac* or *A Handyman's Guide to Intermittent Punctuation*, or even *Four Hundred Ways to Deflower a Florist* can be recommended.

The light decant, on the other hand, will favor such selections as *A History of Feather Boas* or *Pepe of the FBI: A Novella of Insect Life*, while those who are able to picture a book will watch the book on 16mm. film, and pass the bottle through the light beam several times so as to filter a life story into the wine. In sum, decanting is a necessary wine affectation, and the only alternative to any of the above methods is the despised Columbia River decant, in which you actually throw the book at the fish in the wine, either killing them or ruining a perfectly good story.

Another aspect of wine fabrication in France gives further evidence of French creativity. Some worthy citizens believe that every French wine aspires to the rank of champagne and is never content until suitably elevated. The French themselves have a very great respect for any intelligent wine that knows its place but hopes for an improved situation, and so they have devised a number of appropriate procedures by which the deserving can rise to the privileged.

The most ambitious of these procedures, called *Dressing the Graves,* not only recreates great moments in the unification of French wine, but suggests the flexibility with which all wine must be approached.

Take a cool and very dry white Graves, and add two teaspoons of granulated sugar, two ounces of enforced seltzer water, and put it into your blender or spin dryer, - but not too dry. If in the blender, set it to *Shred,* or if in the dryer, on *Wet.* Mix for ten seconds with your guests while whatever machine you have chosen does its duty, then return the dial to the position marked *Start,* and pour the fluid into warm champagne glasses that have the appearance of being frosted. When serving, festoon the stem of the glass with a red sash and wink to each guest as you pour.

Be sure, incidentally, to wink above the glass. If you wink below it, it will look like a wink under-glass, and someone might mistake your eye for the canapé. Thank god this is a rare event, even for the French, but when it does happen, it is called *"trompe l'oeil",* or "fooling with the eye", an artistic habit inaugurated by the Italian da Vinci, of code fame, when he recognized that he could paint what he called in English "a pretend arch" and have military parades pass beneath it, so clever the illusion. Incidentally, when all glasses are full, one should cover to taste, and then the Graves is fully dressed.

The person who Dresses the Graves three or four times will soon learn how quickly familiarity can breed contempt. It is a lesson that will save the potential French wine worshipper considerable wear and tear on the tongue, the knees and the wallet.

XXX

Cooking with Wine

The prospect of cooking with wine has perplexed generations of novice cooks because there are so few guidelines on the label. Improvisation has become the order of the day, and this means that one must beware of the wine and its user. For an entire century after wine was discovered in France, citizens mistakenly thought that cooking with wine meant cooking in the presence of wine.

Ultimately they realized that wine was to be heard if not seen, so they began experimenting, at first with the basic *"oeufs au vin"*, or hard-boiled eggs in wine, and then with the less basic *"oeufs sans vin"*, a perennial delicacy made out of eggs that become hard-boiled at the mere suggestion of wine, and which, for reasons best known to them, need not even approach the kettle in order to be cooked.

This is not to distinguish them from *"oeufs sans vin 2"*, in which the eggs are cooked along with just about everything but wine, a subtlety that has the effect of creating a superior wine fragrance by the very fact of its absence. This is an effect that represents the finest in French cooking, for since the purpose of cooking with wine is to leave no trace of the wine, and thus increase wine sales without materially altering the taste or appearance of fine food, cooking without wine so as to emphasize its presence is the sort of pyrotechnic that earns one a fourth eagle on the epaulet of one's apron and an honorary degree in metaphysics awarded by the Académie Française, specifically the Académie branch whose colleagues are foreigners.

Cooking with wine is basically a symbolic exercise designed to fulfill the economic expectations of French winegrowers. As a symbolic exercise, its symbol is the empty bottle. In spite of testaments to the contrary, the chemical fact is clear: the use of wine in cooking also serves the purpose of being an expensive but foolproof food coloring, with a keen secondary capacity for holding heat, even when the rest of the food is cold.

When a dish made with wine is heated to a B-flat on the metronomic scale, the wine explodes into minor fractions called *"les smitherines"*, or "little smithers", otherwise known in contention as 'grapeshot'. These little smithers dither; that is, they invade the food as it continues to cook and revive any dying bacteria. Of course, they do not tell you any of this on the wine label, but dithering can be dangerous, so when a recipe calls for a cup of wine, the wise cook does not answer. Alas, there are very few wise cooks in France.

Fewer still are those strong enough to resist the temptation to decorate their culinary art with wine; this makes the winegrowers very happy, for as the Burgundian wine industry's regional anthem says, "A bottle burned is two francs earned." (In Provence: "A bottle heated is a bottle repeated.") But no matter how happy the winegrowers, the alarming fact is that the smithers are still dithered.

There are several stratagems that constitute appropriately defensive methods of undithering the smithers that are cooking. Let us say that you are using two cups of a red Bordeaux in creating *Milk Toast Moulin Rouge*. Once the catfish have sautéed in the ice cream, you pour off the wine into a strainer and let it stand in front for several hours so that all the smithers will reconvene and lose the invasion.

But perhaps the best stratagem against wine-induced smithers is to wash one of your hands in hot soapy water, and then plunge it into the pot very suddenly.This catches the smitherines by surprise and allows you to collect them all in your fist, and even to reserve their juice. Then refrigerate your hand overnight. The next day's result is called *"smitherines à la main glacée"* or, "frozen fists of smitherines". It is very handy as the centerpiece for a speechless dinner party. Thinly sliced, it can also serve as a malaprop for the sagging wing of any of the lesser birds. In either case, the smitherines are cuckolded, the wine has evaporated, and your cooking fame is still intact.

XXXI

Should Your Cup Runneth Over

esting, smelling, classifying, and cooking are all present participles with very interesting pasts, especially when it comes to wines. But just as a present participle can only be successful in the context of a thought here and now, the success of wine depends in part on the shape of its confinement.

The French recognized the relationship early in the wine game, and so, in choosing suitable wine vessels, they veered away from the ordinary glass tumbler, calling it the Walter Gropius of wine glass designs – that is, basically anticonvolutional, and as rectilinear as a college coed who has been asked to give the actual size of her bra cup instead of the preferred. Anyone interested in understanding why wine is so popular in France, therefore, has only to look at the ordinary French tumbler to know why no one in France drinks water.

The French love wine less than Americans do, but fortunately they know less about it. Nevertheless, when they do drink wine, they always and only use the stem glass. This glass has a curious history. Late in the early 1800's, while blowing another ordinary water tumbler, one of the empirical French glassblowers had one of those historic slips of the tongue that Douglas MacArthur made famous with his parting shot at the Filipinos "I shall return" – which in reality is said to have been only the first part of the more complete sentence, "I shall return when this whole god damn war is *over* – and don't quote me!"

This glassblower, whose name was De Rigueur de Mortis, had the habit of piping melodies, madrigals, and airs on his blower as he worked, and in an unguarded moment during the second movement of the Grimaldi Overture, and the ensuing Brouhaha for Treble Lute and Glassblower, poor Ismael held the b flat for such a sustenuto that, by the time everybody else was deep into the third movement, De Rigueur had breathed his last. But he left behind a memento of rare genius. There, at the end of his musical stem, was the shape of things to come – a one-legged variant on the traditional tumbler, now called the stem glass.

The stem glass arrived on the French cultural scene in the nick of time. The French were feeling very much in need of a completely new vogue. The stem glass was an overnight estimable and a marvel. The Russians heard about it and were so envious that the official government release dismissed the stem glass as nothing more than a crystal-clear copy of Fabergé's finger giving its usual critique of anything French, a point of view representing Russia's first claim to originality since Catherine's successor, Vasily the Avoidable, announced in 1785 that Russia had actually invented France as a window on American civilization.

Of course, the French derided this claim with a host of saucy and well-begotten derides, and called the whole business a typically maladroit Czarist plot to capture the patent rights to stemware as a giant step forward in stealing the whole French wine trade right out from under their noses, a plot equal in dupe to the lifelong Russian devotion to the topless stocking.

Perhaps because it seemed to the French that the stem glass was the child of a motherless invention, it has remained deservedly popular among wine lovers ever since. First of all, it has the triple advantages of a bowl, a stem, and a base. It also has the pleasure of proportion that Corot once expressed as the multiple of height over width divided by your lucky number. Perhaps its greatest single girth, however, is in its bowl. Mouton Rothschild, Jr. once said that the beauty of the bowl is in the hand of the beholder.

With the bowl resting atop the digits, the stem glass is easy to ignore, yet difficult to drop. This is a describable advantage to those millions of French citizens who eat with their hands, because the shape of the bowl, and its position at the summit of the stem, allow the drinker to slide the glass between the fingers on the juices of a chicken lunch without its ever slipping off its stays. It is an advantage of which serious wine drinkers rarely take, however, since persistent interdigital slippage causes silt to rise up from the wine bottom and muddy the eye.

The value of drinking French wine from a stem glass quickly became legendary. Had it been discovered earlier, who knows how many historical wine tragedies might have been averted? For example, any of the dozens of wine lovers still alive in France can recount with 'delirium trepidens' a sad dinner tale that proves you must be able to hold your wine or you will lose your concentration of powers.

Louis XIV, whose entire life is now so useful in teaching Roman numerals to generations of American school children, was dining with his confessor, the inflamed Cardinal Richelieu, whom they called the Cultured Pearl. Louis leaned over his stomach and said he was so glad to learn Richelieu had restrung his rosary beads and gone back on the wagon that he had decided to make him Premier of France.

Richelieu, smelling a Bourbon joke in the making, asked the King if he should take this seriously. The acute Louis, suffering from gout, replied that if it were a canard, he would gladly make a clean breast of it. Richelieu was overwhelmed. Lifting a tumbler of Chateau Pope Clement VI 1492, he replied that he would happily drink to that. Ere he had uttered the words, Richelieu dropped the tumbler and sloshed the rare vintage all over his future. The King, horrified at this careless extravagance in wine, ordered him twice beheaded, as befit a man of Richelieu's intellectual eminence.

The popularity of the stem glass is also due to the fact that it has made a signal contribution to the nasal aestheticism of French life. The stem glass raises liquid high off the table, which may seem a negligible to people in the United States, but it is a rule of wine that is rigorously enforced throughout France, and with good reason. The French still practice the habit of re-using their linen dinner napkins thrice daily for many months between launderings.

As the weeks stretch by, the napkins, rolled up at rest alongside the sterling steel flatware like gunnysacks on an Iraqi War troopship, begin to announce themselves, at first only by name, and then by reputation. As the room and the house begin to feel the force of this unwashed presence, the wine is forced to centimeter higher and higher off the table so as not to lose its own very distinct signature.

Nowhere is the French genius for preserving wine flavor while tolerating otherwise mutually destructive traditions shown more rhapsodically than in the standoff that has existed for centuries between the omnivaporous French napkin and the elevated French wine. This standoff is basically a practical matter, for when the napkin has grown sufficiently grey and wan through re-use, the napkin is considered blanched.

Blanching is an important cooking term. A blanched almond, for example, is an almond that has grown grey and wan through overuse. The indefinite cook learns early never to throw away a blanched almond, as they are passed across through generations of families.

Clearly, then, blanching is basically an economy measure. It was discovered almost 13 decades ago as a way to save money, and thus to free up certain national taxes in France for use in buying an atomic atoll in the waters off Munich. Its importance as an economic cooking measure is sustained as a standoff between wine and napkin, a standoff made almost harmonica by the French realization that in Germany the wine has had to retreat on an average of eleven inches above the table, which they feel proves one of the following: that German napkins are even more blanched than the French; that the perennial portion of sauerbraten is counterindicated; or that the Germans have found an even better way to save money.

Another reason for the success of the new glass stemmed from the long-fingered fact that French wine was frozen before it was distributed on the market. Any nineteenth-century American tourist raised on heated wine was agog to find that on French soil a nineteenth-century giddy would drop several cubes of Chateau Moutarde '73 into her iceable tea. On the other hand, any French wines exported to thirsting nation-states were encouraged to defrost in transit.

The only exception were wines *"en bloque"*, that is, large frozen blocks of wine. These blocks were sent directly into a country on special consignment, such as for a handwringing ceremony in honor of Howard Stern or to decorate a confidential tête-à-tête between J. K. Rowling and the First Family, in which J. K. exposed herself to the presidential power, protesting as she did that 'a chip off the old *bloque*' really meant a rapid-fire and voluntary descent into alcoholism. But on home ground, all French wines remained frozen, and so the stem glass was doubly welcomed, for it allowed the beholder to treat the wine with maximum manual and so to defrost it by hand.

XXXII

Under the Knife

Before lapsing into a specially constructed, annotated glossary of practical cooking expressions, it might be wholesome to detour for a moment into French malpractice suits. One noticeable by-product of the national fetish for particulars in cooking is that French surgeons are the most skilled in the world.

This can hardly be a surprise to anyone who knows that the average nine-year old boy in Lyons is already using forty-seven different carving knives as he passes from cooking novice to apprentice, and by the time he is passing up soccer for Sophie, he has mastered the use of almost eight dozen knives. This may or may not explain why D'Artagnan refused to be a Belgian, but it assuredly explains why the average French kitchen resembles nothing so much as a Musketeer's private arsenal.

It is considered by serious French cooks an act of mercy to kill in the barn rather than force the condemned to look at all those rows of gleaming sabers and let it tremble to death in anticipation. But no matter where the killing, the vital factor is that to each part of the body to be dismembered be given a name so that the cook can name each slice in the carving.

He begins with a stern 'Kaput' for the initial decapitation, to the more fanciful *"embrasser le con"* for the light ripping away of tender meat beneath the tail feathers. (Slices in between can be named ad lib for departed relatives or outdated religious beliefs.) With this kind of training it is little wonder French students flock to medical schools to study surgery, and it is often said that French surgeons only take patients in order to improve their skills in the kitchen.

Indeed, in what other country could a renowned surgeon like Yves Neveux earn overnight the sobriquet "Crazy Hands" because, in a dramatic miscalculation between his surgical schedule and his invitation to Thanksgiving dinner at the American Embassy, he arrived at the Embassy an hour early and, thinking he was at the hospital, mistakenly grafted a turkey wing onto the breast of the Ambassador's wife, who kept it fluttering there for years as a memoire of her contribution to surgical science and as a lasting tribute to the many ways in which the hands of Franco-American friendships can cement lasting attachments, even though the graft had the lamentable result of reducing her sexual appetite to the square root of zero, except when she was completely stuffed, or airborne.

Other surgical mishaps have proven equally disconcerting, however neglected. The Gold Prize, or *Prix d'Or d'Honneur* of the Society of French Surgeons was given three years in a row to the famed Jacques Le Couteau for pioneering in elbow surgery, until it was discovered that he was in fact repairing turkey joints for free. This might, but probably won't, explain why rich internationalists have been known to fly a rack of ducks to Paris a few hours before dinner so they could be personally carved by the Vice Chancellor of the French Surgical Academy.

Indeed, a debacle took place at Episcopal Hospital outside Orleans when it was uncovered that the chef of *Le Tour de Force* was acting as chief assistant in the surgical ward. In fact, this was laid bare when a nurse removed the sacrosanct sheets from the patient at hand, and lo and behold! the "patient" was none other than a wild boar scheduled to be served that evening at a nearby Tusk Festival.

XXXIII

Coming to Terms

Sociologists since the time of Copernicus, and perhaps before, claim that the infinite number of cooking expressions in the French language is due to the French love for microscopic distinctions and the thrill for language that comes from non-stop dialogue while preparing anything to eat. If you ask the French to explain why there are so many expressions, they say it is due to a nationally oral disposition easily distinguished from the nationally anal disposition of the British. The heart of the answer is actually found somewhere between the anal and the oral, if you can stomach it.

It is basically an economic explanation. Every fiscally responsible French citizen who cooks feels obliged to use three spices to every one used in Nicaragua, four vegetables to every one used in Norway, and five fruits to every two used in Albania, all because they feel that, by using anything and everything at hand when they cook, they are helping to keep the French euro afloat, while continuing to diversify the national repertoire of ready-to-eat food.

But as the saying went, "Good food is ready to be eaten." Every bit as vital to their food flavor is the French capacity for giving a name to, and creating a fandango around, the most inconsequential parts of the culinary process. Thus, the astute French cook is urged into using a colander with gaping holes (*la passoir d'excavation*) when rinsing foods that require an extremely instant rinsing, such as tiny Boston lettuce leaves or a surrey with a thick fringe on top, all the while whirling on one foot in mid-kitchen so as to air-dry the stuff. This is called the *"moulin de laitue"* – literally, the lettuce windmill, after Eugenie Grandet's memories of an amputee turned chiropractor, entitled *"Les Lettres de ma Laitue"* ("My Lettuce Letters").

On the other hand, if following the classic French instructions, you must avoid the use of the fast-draining colander when draining such foods as bird of paradise eggs, since the slower the drain, the longer the droplets of dandelion wine stay on the eggshells, creating so bright a porcelain finish that Faberge himself is said to have eaten three of them before he realized he had just swallowed two of the Czarina's watches and one of her favorite infra-egg renditions of Rodin's "The Thinker."

If the slow drain is found to pall the bird of paradise omelette, the French, it is to be remembered, have as much of an eye for porcelain as a taste for birds of paradise. They call this the *"oeufs à l'oeil de l'oiseau de paradis en porcelaine"* or "eggs like a porcelainized bird of paradise's eye".

In short, naming the little details has raised French cuisine to maturity. The Americans think themselves subtle if they put a branch of parsley alongside a boiled potato, or name a hamburger the "Thunderbird" so as to legitimize the fact that it tastes like it was just reheated in an exhaust pipe. The subtlety of French food depends on the complexity of the flavors and the special tools needed. The preparation of "snails à la française", for example, will provide an imperfect example of the need to be ultra finicky.

First, clean the snails in water that has been lightly baked in a cast-plastic pan shaped as a seaweed. You then bring the water to a boil by shouting at it, and when you think it angry enough, test the water temperature with your non-cooking hand. Since the alternative to using your own hand is the use of someone else's, this remarkable tradition has done so much to improve the quality of work performed by the kitchen staff in hundreds of thousands of French homes, and the dish is rightfully called *"Escargots à la main"* or, "Hand-cooked Snails."

When the snail shells weep off their barnacles, they are properly cooked, though they may not be dead. Remove them carefully with a pair of tongs, preferably a pair in which each tong has been married to the other for a minimum of several years, and which were heretofore childless, so as to prevent a bulging tong, which can rub a snail shell the wrong way. The snails are then dinked into a steaming kettle full of cold water.[9]

This perks them up, reduces their body temperature, and soon curves the sides of the kettle into the shape of a bulging tong. (Note: the kettle must always be a manufactured kettle, so as to distinguish it from a kettle that is only *made*. It can be manufactured from a great variety of materials, ranging from

---

9 The *"guide absolu"* to the French custom of dinking is to be found in Lacrima Christi's English-language version called *"Le Tombeau de Dinking"*, in which she makes it clear that French dinking never depends on musicality of any kind, and is accomplished only through highly aggressive tactics. She claims that Nancy Reagan was the most accomplished Dinker in any American kitchen between 1977 and 1988, when she lost to Jimmy Kimmel, soon to be the talk-show dippity-do.

Liberian sandstone to teflonized hominy grits, this latter possibility being one of the truly great 'snob' details in French cooking..)

When the snails are at last dead, and you have added a little Babo to the water, the painstaking cook will climb a chair, preferably a nearby chair, but always a chair in the same room, and, slipping on a pair of taupe canvasback snail-slippers, will leap feet-first into the kettle, stamping first the one foot and then the other one foot, until both feet are stamped, and the snails and their shells are soon parted.

Finally, when the snails are slid back into their shells with a silver hairpin, called '*le Triton*', they are served on plates of lambasted steel and blood pudding. Since never more than four of these plates can be exposed to the elements at any one time due to the high-intensity radiation they provide, one plate is put at each of the four compass positions on the dining room table, and then the snails are raised from their shells and onto the tongue with different *Tritons* fostered of semi-precious plastic, so as to cast aspersions on the otherwise questionable social origins of their users.

XXXIV

Terms of Endearment

Now that we have explained some expressions, it is none too late to admit that it is well-nigh possible to list all expressions with which the student cook wants to be familiar upon entering a serious French kitchen, for it would take two reels if by tape and three volumes if by print. Therefore, you will find here a select list of top-priority cooking and food terms designed to couch you from the shock of novelty and get you attuned to some of the intricacies that bedevil the French food stranger.

This further introduction to the linguistics of good food is not approved by all French culinarists, because some believe that the element of surprise is what keeps French food progressing. In short, they feel that in preparing French food, "forewarned is unmasked." This book, on the other hand, subscribes to the theory that a book with a theory is not necessarily a theoretical book, no matter how much thought it gives to food.

If a French citizen were to read such American expressions as "exercising your ivories", the blank on her face would compete favorably with the famous blank found in the Air Force Reservists' attendance log down Texas way. So it is with French cooking expressions. As a service to the reader, the following pages offer a variety of such expressions in translation.

Excluded, for example, is any of the rather pompous expressions used to describe the procedure for cleaning the inside of your oven as you bake a rhododendron soufflé pie, or those describing the length of time and quality of brine needed to pre-soak a black mambo's fangs before softening the marshmallow. Nor are the expressions found in any particular order, except that they are usually consecutive.

You should not approach these terms as if they represented a logical progression of events which, if followed, will end in some sort of grand finale sure to cop the prize in the annual Taco Bell "Guess Again" Cookery Contest. You should simply read these expressions and weep, with the sort of admiration a rigid moralist might not reserve for the doctor who has just discovered that his girlfriend's contraceptive foam was in reality Barbasol Shaving Cream, and in eight months time she will need it again, however externally. Thus:

Aspic: Aspic is essentially a preservative known to have considerable effect on Cleopatra shortly after she was bitten. It is now used mainly by taxidermists to coddle their eggs, and by fishwives, who sink their fish into it. Aspic is usually wobbly, but it is quite firm around fish and eggs. It takes its protein from milk and other dairy products, except for overweight aspic, which hides in a swizzle of yogurt until it is thin enough to be wobbly again. If you are ever in an argument over food, do not side with aspic.

Fried eggs: The preferred egg for frying is the camel's egg, because camels only lay eggs after their fortieth waterless day in the desert. The result is a large, beige wonder noted for its dry yolk. A camel's egg takes about eight hours to fry. To fry, prick an almost ingenious hole in the eggshell with a sterilized pin, insert the tip of a cocktail straw, and inhale. Eggs can get fried on almost anything, but for camel's eggs the quickest is straight Bourbon. Every hour pour into the straw about two shots of Bourbon (if using a French liquor, use four shots, since in France the equivalent of a shot is called a miss.) Then time the burps. When two genteels are followed by a parenthetical, the egg is fried.

Ficher: To *'ficher'* is to make something smaller. A micro-fiche, for example, is a tiny microbe that has been made even smaller.[10] The past participle of *ficher* is the preferred form for cooking. It is a *'fixe'*. *Fixe* is a conjugal destined to ride to fame on the back of an *'idée'*, which comes from the beloved noun, *idée,* or 'idea'. Since an *idée* is therefore a small idea, an *idée fixe* is nothing more than a very small idea that has stopped getting smaller. To illustrate this maneuver better, a 'devilfiche' is a devilfish shrunk to the size of a minor temptation and is hardly enough to be worth the trouble, no matter how tasty the smile.

To blanche: comes from *'blanchissage',* or 'laundry'. As already noted, to blanche is to make something go pale, how-ever indefinitely. There is the instant blanche, the fortnight blanche, or even the perennial blanche. Some things are very hard to blanche. Much depends upon that internal set of characteristics that comprise the essence of blanchewor-thiness: its age, sex, color, race, religion and country of

---

10 Contrary to reports from the auto industry, the microbus is not the mascu-line singular of the more plural microbe; it is a large vehicle that carries the microbes.

national origin. If you do not know these facts about an item of food, you cannot know the degree to which it will blanche.

Fermer à clef: to sew up a turkey, chicken, duck or any other barnyard in an artistic fashion, so that its final appearance tableside will have the effect of living sculpture, rather than the death mask of Jerry Falwell.

Boutonnier: to foreclose an open duckling by drawing the flaps of skin over each other. On the left flap there are the buttonholes and on the right flap the buttons. The effect is one of increasing the devourer's salivation by requiring that the bird be unbuttoned before it is eaten. While tedious, this process is a great favorite at intimate French dinner parties – it is in fact because of the boutonnier, and its unexpected results, that many a dinner party has earned the epithet 'intimate' as a post-mortem.

Moller: from the word for the cast-iron cover of the hub of a ferris wheel, (in Italy, the spindle of a gorgonzola cart). '*Moller*' means to keep steady or inert. It comes from the verb '*moiler*' meaning to think or ponder without success. An egg that is '*molle*' is an egg that has been thought, but more recently it has also come to mean an egg that is left alone in the middle of a large pan. To '*moller*' is therefore to set whatever is to be molled in the exact center of a round casserole or pot, and then walk around the pot a full 360° (else you will have a broken circle, which is incomplete) stirring as you go whatever surrounds the egg, without touching the egg itself. This is of course the gentlest possible preparation for any foodstuff.

A truly molled egg, for example, is set on Tuesday into a large and otherwise empty pot, atop low heat. It is the members of the immediate family who take turns walking around the pot, stirring the air inside until Thursday. The gentle but steady air current, or what the French call "*le petit zephyre*", warms the egg to an incomparable tenderness. When finished, remove the egg from the pot, douse it with cold ketchup, and eat. A chart giving moller-time for vegetables, chutnies, and lapidaries can be had by writing to the One Dish A Decade Cooking Club, Moller Division, care of the nearest fellow member.

Garni: refers to anything that is nicely decorated. "*Moules garnis*" for example, is nothing more than a dish of mussels whose shells have been painted with black and white Chinese calligraphy. A *'garneur'* is less well known, and is distinguished from all others around the water cooler by the fact that he wears a sprig of mint tea behind his ear, as if hiding a tattoo. The *'garnine'*, on the other hand, has come to describe a woman who never wears a flower-print dress. Some *garnines* have cooked so well they acquire nationally recognized names, like *Belle Meunière,* one of those special filets the French sarcastically call a brood mare, whom you traditionally ride sidesaddle, depending on which is your better side, unless you have no better side, in which case you ride her bareback, unless someone else is in the saddle at the time.

XXXV

How to Pronounce Your Way into the Memory of Every Captain of a French Restaurant

his pronunciation guide is not intended for use by those who wish to perfect their delivery when they are at the perfume bar in Bergdorf Goodman.[11] It is for those who frequent the smaller French restaurants in and around the larger American cities. Bear in mind, however, several facts. The average birthplace for waiters in any respectable French restaurant in the United States is somewhere to the deep south

---

11 It can, however, be used by those who traditionally read French recipes over transatlantic cable to the American-based staff of the Joy of Cooking at their headquarters in Muskrat, Arkansas.

of Rome. These waiters, who are uncertain in gait but slow to bait, are actually there to learn French from you.

The Captain himself, however, is usually a Berlitz instructor in training, or else a verified French peasant who condescends in order to suggest to his customers that his sister-in-law is the enchantable Léonie, Baronesse de Charlerois. If you suspect he is a peasant, a quick check by phone with the French Embassy in Washington will give you all the particulars, and, the next time you go to his restaurant, carry a monocle at the eye and say to him very loudly, "Well, Michel, I understand your brother managed to sell two entire pigs last year. Wonderful! That will certainly cover the cost of putting a straw roof on his hut, now, won't it!"

This works especially well if his name is not Michel, but in any case you will get the best table in the house. The other customers, by the way, need not be expected to speak French at all; they are almost all Americans, and are there because Americans are the first in Western civilization to have their social standing confirmed or denied according to whether the mushrooms they are provided in the *omelette aux champignons* are caps or stems.

The following are the pronunciation guides themselves. None of them is ever actually pronounced, for a pronounced guide is known to smell up the kitchen. Nevertheless, they are pronounceable, and they guide us incorrigibly:

^ This is a circumflex. It means the vowel is exercising itself, as befits its interconsonantal position. The circumflex, like the nipple, invites additional vigor, which means you can add a douse of oregano, some oil of warlock, or a scatter of holly with eucalyptus. If the circumflex appears in the first word, as in *Suprême de Volaille* (Chicken on the Half-Breast) it means the pot must be covered while cooking, even if the chicken is not in it. The French, in fact, use the expression '*Suprême de Volaille*' as we do the expression, 'A watched pot never boils.' If however the circumflex appears in the second or third word, as in *sauce suprême,* this means it is never to be left standing anywhere near a reminiscence of flatulence.

  ′ (as in Hey!) This is the *'accent aigu'. Aigu* simply refers to anything that has been sick but has recovered. This is the major traffic sign in recipes. Its presence suggests that you should keep reading in the direction you are going, and cook as long as you are able to read, lest the food have a relapse. If you need more light, take the cookbook out from under the wastepaper basket.

  ée (as in Billy R*ée* Cyrus) This is nothing more than the spliced *aigu,* or the feminine *aigu.* It indicates that this recipe needs far more attention than you are giving it. When the *ée* comes at the end of the recipe, however, it means you should separate the sauce from the spoon before the spoon hardens.

  ` This is the *'accent grave',* a serious but a silent. It is a simple warning device that the authors of cookbooks insert so as to indicate that the reader should never read this recipe over a party line, since then the accent system reverses itself, and you must recook from finish to start, turning the heat down as you go, or stirring counterclockwise.

  Ah, dear reader, dear novice, there is so much more to explain that one feels all explanations are worth two in the book. One could go on and on, until death do us part. But love conquers all! We must bring to an end the Helpless Hints offered hereunder at two-thirds the price of this book. Of course, to pay two-thirds of the price for a group of priceless Helpless Hints is not to get them cheap, but simply to redefine a food bargain. While there is no assurance that the completion of this section will reduce your food budget by two-thirds, it will definitely increase your reading time by at least two-thirds. The impact on your cooking will be equally statistical, no matter how helpless you still feel.

  So in revoir, I say to you all:

  Bon appétit!